Ghost Buck

THE LEGACY OF ONE MAN'S
FAMILY AND ITS
HUNTING TRADITIONS

We love the outdoors! More great titles from Islandport Press.

Birds of a Feather by Paul J. Fournier
Leave Some for Seed by Tom Hennessey
Backtrack by V. Paul Reynolds
A Life Lived Outdoors by George Smith
Where Cool Waters Flow by Randy Spencer

These and other books are available at:
www.islandportpress.com.

Islandport Press is a dynamic, award-winning publisher
dedicated to stories rooted in the essence and sensibilities of
New England. We strive to capture and explore the grit, beauty,
and infectious spirit of the region by telling tales, real and
imagined, that can be appreciated in many forms by readers,
dreamers, and adventurers everywhere.

Ghost Buck

THE LEGACY OF ONE MAN'S
FAMILY AND ITS
HUNTING TRADITIONS

By Dean B. Bennett

Foreword by Robert Kimber

ISLANDPORT PRESS

Islandport Press
P.O. Box 10
247 Portland Street
Yarmouth, Maine 04096
www.islandportpress.com
books@islandportpress.com

ISBN: 978-1-939017-66-6
Library of Congress Card Number: 2014959681

Dean L. Lunt, publisher
Book jacket design, Karen F. Hoots / Hoots Design
Book design, Michelle A. Lunt / Islandport Press
Cover photograph courtesy of the author
Back cover photograph courtesy of the Bennett family

In memory of my grandfather,
Jason Ransom Bennett

and

Others also now gone—
Donald Bennett
Elden Hathaway
Robert Farrington
Ronald Martin

and

to my family
Cheryl and Chuck, my steady hunting companions;
Rick, who has hunted with me since he was a boy; and
Nathaniel and Abigail, who promise the future.

Other Books by Dean B. Bennett

Allagash: Maine's Wild and Scenic River
Nature and Renewal: WIld River Valley and Beyond
The Wilderness from Chamberlain Farm:
A Story of Hope for the American Wild
The Forgotten Nature of New England:
A Search for the Traces of the Original Wilderness
Maine's Natural Heritage

The fundamental things apply,
As time goes by.[1]

—from "As Time Goes By" (1931)

Acknowledgments

I thank my daughter, Cheryl; my son-in-law, Charles (Chuck) Martin; my son, Richard (Rick); and my wife, Sheila, for their encouragement and help in making this book. I also thank Blaine Mills, historian of Greenwood, Maine, for his many contributions to this book, and his wife, Margie, for her help. I thank, too, my friend, Robert Kimber, a true outdoorsman, for writing the foreword and swapping deer hunting stories with me after every season. I extend special appreciation to my editor, Genevieve Morgan of Islandport Press, for seeing the broader meaning of this story, and helping me bring it to the public.

And finally, I express my appreciation to the Ghost Buck, for stirring the imaginations of deer hunters everywhere, in whatever manifestation it may take. I must acknowledge that when writing about it here, my own imagination may have been, at times, over-stirred. But what is a good deer story without some embellishment?

(Author's note: Unattributed quoted material is from the Camp Sheepskin register.)

Table of Contents

Foreword

If the title of this memoir, Ghost Buck, has drawn you to
this book expecting to read about deer hunting in Maine
and a monster buck who always seems to dissolve into thin
air before a hunter's very eyes, you will not be disappointed.
Hunting deer has been a central pursuit in Dean Bennett's life
and one he has devoted himself to with the dedication and
elan he brings to any enterprise he undertakes. But it is the
subtitle, The Legacy of One Man's Family and Their Hunting
Traditions, that suggests both the greater scope and depth of
this memoir.

Dean can trace his ancestry back to at least nine generations who have lived in the rugged, forested hill country of
Greenwood, Maine, for over two hundred years. He was born
and raised in the village of Locke's Mills in the northeastern
corner of Greenwood Township; and in 1936, when Dean
was just a year old, his father and grandfather, assisted by
thirty-seven friends and relatives, built their deer camp in one
marathon day. Camp Sheepskin, which took its name from
nearby Sheepskin Bog, served not only as a hunting camp for
Dean's grandfather, father, and uncles, as well as for family
friends, but it was also the extended Bennett family's getaway
for weekends and holidays throughout the year, the scene of
cookouts and birthday parties and the place where Dean as a
boy became a passionate and keen observer of plant and animal life, began developing his skills as a nature photographer,

and, at age fourteen, joined his elders in their annual deer hunts. At that place he loved and among people he loved, he put down his roots and spread his wings. Camp Sheepskin and the country around it is where Dean set out on his path to becoming the eloquent spokesman for the wild world he has become.

Anyone who knows Dean knows he is a jack of innumerable trades and master of them all. Dilettantism has no place in his vocabulary. Tally up all the things he has done superbly and you have enough careers for half a dozen men, not just one: professional cabinet maker, industrial arts teacher, high-school science teacher, designer of environmental-education curricula for Maine public schools, professor of environmental studies and education at the University of Maine at Farmington, author of seven books on Maine and New England natural history and wilderness preservation.

Dean is not content to pursue anything just halfway. When he decided he'd like to write some books for children, too, he took courses in children's literature and in writing children's books; and when he then decided he might as well illustrate his books himself, he took courses in drawing and painting with oils, acrylics, and watercolors and continued his lifelong studies in nature photography. The fruits of these "hobbies," which he has taken to high professional levels, add a rich visual dimension to his books, whether for adults or children.

Whatever arts and skills Dean decides to learn, he learns not by gritting his teeth and buckling down, but with a sense that nothing else could be more fun in the world than what he is learning right now, that the hours and energy he invests in these disciplines do not drain him but, on the contrary, enliven and inspire him. Through the written word and images captured with his camera, pencil, and paintbrush, he has conveyed to others the beauty of the natural world and civilization's dependence on the wild as its source of vitality, health, and renewal.

As this memoir makes eminently clear, Dean has thrived from earliest childhood in the company of family and friends and in Camp Sheepskin's world of mountains, bogs, and forest where whitetail deer still roam. No wonder he has returned there for nearly every deer season over the last sixty-six years. The father and grandfather who mentored him there are gone, and now he is both father and grandfather himself, hunting with his son and daughter and teaching their children the ways of deer and the ways of men and women who hunt those deer—including that ever elusive ghost buck—with respect and gratitude.

Robert Kimber
Temple, Maine
June 2014

Preface

Every year the mill shut down for a reason that most have forgotten, or never knew. Of the few that have heard of it, some would snicker, others would think it absurd, and there are those today who would bluntly, even angrily, say that the reason was immoral. But back then, more than a century ago, the opening day of deer hunting season was at the top of everyone's mind, like cream in the bottle of milk delivered every morning to the back porch.

As the day drew near, everybody joked about how their trigger finger was beginning to crook up, and went around saying the same thing I heard my father say a half-century later—"There hain't no deer"—just to keep people away from places where everyone knew they hunted. And then there was the big buck that left huge tracks, long rubs and gouges way up on trees, and big piles of large droppings, tempting people to compare it in size to a small moose. Of course, no one had seen the monster deer in recent memory . . . not clearly, anyway. For that matter, no one could say for sure that he or she had *ever* seen it. Still, it was only a matter of time before it would be brought into town by some lucky hunter. So it was understandable why, on the big day, with the idea of hunting flashing like a neon sign in everybody's mind, so many people called in sick or had some kind of crisis, or just plain disappeared, so that the mill couldn't function.

The act of shutting down the mill wasn't any small, trivial indicator of where deer hunting stood in people's minds. Never mind that the E. L. Tebbetts Spool Company mill was the major industry in town, the largest employer, the biggest part of the area's economy. Even the town, Locke's Mills, was named after the mill and its original owner, Samuel Locke. People came from all over the area to work in the mill, paying heed to the whistle that told them they had but ten minutes left before the mill started up at seven a.m., and a blast right on the dot of that time, saying they should begin work. After eight hours of labor, the whistle blew again and they left for home, their hearing numbed by the loud machinery and flapping belts, minds pressed down by the tedium of endless repetitive activity, and bodies aching and exhausted—all for barely enough money to meet the necessities of life, money they needed to survive.

But when hunting season rolled around, never mind the need to work or the demands of the mill; it was more important to hunt deer than pay attention to the damn whistle.

Many have tried to explain this phenomenon. I've been asked from time to time why I hunt. I've never had a good answer because I never thought about it much. It was something I grew up doing, and I took it for granted that this was just something my family did in the normal course of our lives, as did many other families in my town. I have hunted deer for nearly seven decades now, and, on occasion, even absented myself from my own job responsibilities to pursue the white-tails, just as my ancestors did at the E. L. Tebbetts Spool Company mill.

Most everyone will tell you that *Why do you hunt?* is a complicated psychological and sociological question, without a simple answer. But after a lifetime of experiencing this urge, which lurks in the back of my mind throughout the winter, after the fall hunt, and then begins a restless squirming in spring that gradually worms its way into my consciousness as summer progresses, awakening into an overpowering longing with the first smell of dying leaves in the fall, I think I've finally found the answer—for me, anyway.

If you are someone who doesn't hunt, you may see parallels here with something in your own life that you love to do year after year—something that occupies your memories, daily thoughts, and plans for the future, something that bonds you with family and friends, and something that adds its little bit to the character of your community, and, on a large scale, to the collective culture in which you live.

But if you are someone whose very existence is gripped every fall by an irresistible urge to hunt deer, you will see more than parallels: You will see yourself here. And if you pursue this passion in a special place where you've gone as long as you can remember, you will find a deeper meaning in this story—a meaning drawn from the simple pleasure of connecting with yourself, with others, and with a certain place in nature, and with one of its creatures of grace and beauty: the white-tailed deer, an animal interwoven into the fabric of our culture, particularly so for those in rural areas who have a long line of ancestral connection.

My ancestral connection to deer hunting began with my grandfather, Jason Ransom Bennett. Through him that connection was enlarged to include his family and myself, and because of this, I have a better grasp of the position deer hunting holds in our culture, especially in rural communities; its place in the geography of the landscape; and its place in the mind. It's in the mind where the story reveals how hunting can lead one to contemplate the meaning of our relationship to the deer and, by extension, the rest of nature, for the act of hunting can do this, especially when it ends in a death.

One thing that made it possible to write this book is the primary source material I had available. First, I interviewed my grandfather extensively in 1953 for a high school assignment, when he was in his early sixties, and have always kept that information. Second, my family handed down many letters, diaries, and photographs, beginning with my grandfather's mother, Mary Bennett. She was born in 1866, and I knew her well because she lived close by until her death, when I was a senior in high school. Third, ever since I was one year old, my family's experiences have been recorded, often in great detail, in three volumes of the register of Camp Sheepskin, my family's small, unassuming, wood-framed, two-room building located on a ninety-acre lot of land in a heavily wooded and hilly area of western Maine. In the pages of this record, I found the reason why deer hunting has been such a constant in my life. This register chronicles my family's relationship with a place of respite, a place where I spent many days during my boyhood and as a young man, especially with my grandfather.

From the time my grandfather built the camp more than three-quarters of a century ago, six generations of my family have visited during all months of the year. The fall deer hunting season always held a special attraction, however, and it remains so today. Through that span of time, deer hunting underwent many changes in our family, as it did in society at large. Those changes are seen here in human terms—in the context of one family's experience.

My grandfather was a well-loved figure, respected for his honesty, sense of humor, and the caring and love he gave to his family. These character traits were also appreciated by those in the community. He was the town tax collector, an unenviable job that one could only keep if people thought they were being treated honestly, fairly, and respectfully, and one earned by the votes of residents at the annual town meeting, where folks had the chance to say their piece, and usually did. He was voted into the position each year for twenty-seven years, and over that time the citizens of my community came to know and like him for these qualities, as well as for his pleasant manner and interesting and entertaining conversation. People would come to his home to pay their taxes and then stay for an hour or more, visiting. I know this because I grew up right next door and was often there when people came, listening in and enjoying his abundant stories.

My grandfather was my best friend in my boyhood, and later, when I was a young man, my best hunting companion. Through him I learned that among the many encounters hunters have with deer, there is usually at least one that is told and progressively enlarged upon until it moves from a mere story to the status of a legend, sometimes with mythical overtones. For this reason one should read this book thoughtfully, as one would do when trying to separate fact from fiction—especially so with my grandfather's Ghost Buck.

Dean B. Bennett
Mount Vernon, Maine

Prologue

I hear a stick break and become all eyes and ears. A thump. The sounds come from below my stand, toward the bog. Something walking—heavy. There's movement in a clump of small firs at the edge of the bog. It's still in deep shade down there in the undergrowth. A pounding on the ground. Some tree limbs seem to move through the shadows. A massive rack of antlers? Is it my imagination? A huge, dark form— only an instant of inky blackness. It becomes quiet. Then, a deer blows, high-pitched, intense, angry. It's strangely unsettling, and surprises me. A loud crash, and silence follows— except for my thumping heart.

I snap my head up and look around. Nothing appears to have changed, except that the sun over the mountains seems a little higher. Had I nodded off? Had I been dreaming? I'd been awake since three o'clock in the morning, ever since I'd built the fire in the cookstove to warm up the camp and get the coffee water boiling. We'd joked about the Ghost Buck over breakfast. "This is the year we'll see it," I'd said. "I can feel it in my bones."

"It's just your arthritis," Chuck, my son-in-law, had said, and we all laughed.

I'm alert now, listening. There's a faint rustling. I cock my head and strain to hear. There it is again, more definite.

I shift my position in the stand to look around, trying to determine the sound's direction. It's up by the Old Cellar.

Then a patch of orange, and Chuck comes into sight. He sees me and waves. I wave back, relaxed. It's been a morning of memories.

That's one of the main reasons why I come back to the camp and these woods, year after year. It's a place where I can once again bring back the people and events in my past that have meant so much to me. Each year I leave knowing what's important—that there is a continuity provided by the camp and the surrounding country, passed on to each new generation. This is its legacy. I have been fortunate to have one place that has remained relatively unchanged, to which I have been able to return freely throughout my years on this earth, in the company of those close to me—all of us bound together, with a Ghost Buck to stir our imaginations.

CHAPTER ONE

The Shadagee Deer

Heard some shots over toward Shadagee.
—NOVEMBER 7, 1953, CAMP SHEEPSKIN REGISTER

The gaslight shining through the camp window is now behind me, and as I step out into the morning darkness of opening day, I'm thinking about the letter we'd received, more than a decade ago in the year 2000. Although many years have passed since I first read it, I still think about it. There was a chance that we could have lost our hunting privileges on this land that I'm about to step on.

I cross the Old County Road, the root of the issue we had faced, and keep going. Soon it's what the shadows might be hiding that I'm thinking about. The headlamp casting the shadows only emphasizes the limit of my vision and a mysteriousness that spawns a familiar uneasiness. If I'm honest with myself, I would admit to a little fearfulness as to what might be beyond the wall of darkness penetrated fleetingly here and there by the light of my headlamp. I'm steeled for the unexpected *thud* of something jumping out at me, or the pounding of something running on the frozen ground, or even a set of

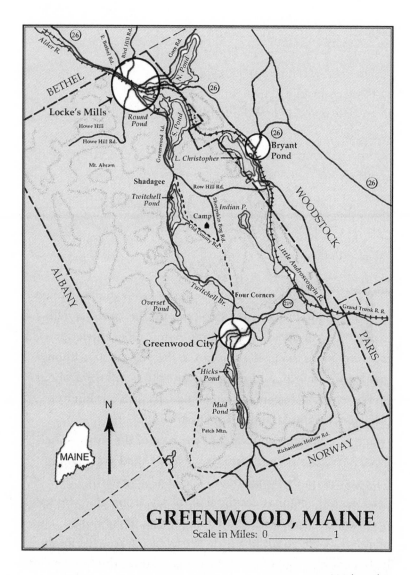

Map by author

Map of Greenwood, Maine

staring eyes caught in the light—perhaps those of the mystical Ghost Buck that haunts us here. I don't quite understand it, but I take some perverse enjoyment from the effect of being in these dark woods, and have always looked forward to it.

I follow the overgrown wood road that dips down into a wet place, still showing ruts from trucks that hauled timber from a cut. I hike up to the top of the knoll by the Old Potato Field, where seventy-five-year-old white pines now replace potatoes as a crop, stepping lightly on the crackling leaves as the road gradually descends to a trickling brook. A culvert has been pulled here, and a berm bulldozed by the lumber company to prevent vehicles from entering the area. I slog through a swampy section at the end of Sheepskin Bog, step over another tiny brook and berm, creep up a small hill toward the Old Cellar, to a previously placed white birch limb visible in the darkness. Here, I turn left, stepping gingerly over the scattered boulders of an old stone wall, and walk blindly for a short distance through small firs along the edge of what was once a skidder trail. Soon, I reach the tree and the stand that we put in place yesterday. It has taken me twenty minutes in a darkness illuminated by a lifetime of familiarity.

I turn off my light and begin to climb by feel in the dark. When I look up, I see black lines etched against a transparent celestial blue. They hover wildly overhead, like the gesture drawing I did in an art course more than twenty-five years ago. Professor Higgins had told me how to get this effect: "Use free movement, and relate to your subject in an emotional way; draw what you sense it's trying to do. Feel the vitality you see in your subject, and keep your pencil on the paper the whole time."

I know I couldn't have done it better than this oak, sharply inscribing itself into the clear, crisp, predawn sky. Its skeletal, leafless limbs reach out, leaf-barren for only a few days—a stark end to a wrenching alteration of the tree's solar machinery that started when the first deep chill swept over the forest. The oak's leaves had first blotched brown and red, twig ends had weakened, and then the inevitable: A fall storm had violently stripped them away. What I see above me is an expression of the enduring nature I feel about this place. The oak tree has scribbled itself into a drawing that would have made my art teacher happy.

I move upward. The coldness of the ladder's steel rungs penetrates my gloves. Finally, with numbing fingers, I grasp the footrest, a brace, then the seat. I reach up and grope for the hook to hang my gun on. Now, with my knees on the footrest, I worm my body through the opening between the armrest and seat, and then, with a contortionist's twist, I'm in the seat facing outward and the tree has become a backrest. Sometimes it seems more trouble than it's worth, but it isn't. Every dawn here brightens my life.

These years I climb trees a little more slowly and carefully, debating whether it's getting more difficult. It's easy to blame the below-freezing temperature and all the clothes I have on, while brushing away the unsettling question of how many more years I can safely climb a tree. Many more, I hope. I put on the safety belt, adjust myself on the padded cushion that I carry behind me, fastened by a strap over my belt, retrieve my gun, and check my watch. It's shooting time. I load my gun, and just as I finish, I hear a gunshot in the distance behind me. It sounded like it was a mile or so away, off in the direction where my grandfather shot his first deer, in a section of town called Shadagee.

I've hunted deer here since I was a boy. My grandfather started hunting this country in the early part of the 1900s. It was here in the 1920s that he taught my father, Donald, how to hunt. In the 1940s and '50s, they both taught me and my brother, James, the skills we needed—taking us hunting around our camp near the bog, named Sheepskin, where I now sit.

Nearly every weekend from May through November during my boyhood years, my family came to the camp, and in the fall, we came to hunt deer. Our hunting trips were enjoyable family events, and often included the company of my grand-mother Cora and my mother, Elsie. Hunting was more than just recreation. Getting a deer was important business. With my father as the single wage earner, working as a laborer in the wood-turning mill, our family didn't have a lot of money. The venison was needed, and every bit of it used. My mother made mincemeat out of the neck every fall that a deer was taken, which found its way into delicious pies.

Hunting was a way of life in these rural hill towns of western Maine, part of the culture. I learned just how deeply it runs in my family from my grandfather, who often told me stories when I was a boy about his own childhood. One was a favorite: "The year I turned sixteen," he would say, "I had been working in the mill, but work got slack, and I got laid off. My grandfa-ther, Ransom Cole, hired me for two hundred dollars and room and board to work for a year on his farm in Shadagee. That November I shot two bucks, the legal limit back then."

Many years passed before I discovered the details of my grandfather's hunting success during that year on his grandfather's farm. I was going through my mother's effects after she died when I came across a letter dated November 19, 1906, from Elvira Cole, my grandfather's grandmother. Elvira had sent the letter to her daughter, my grandfather's mother, Mary, fondly called Maime by her family and friends. Elvira wrote:

> Dear Maime,
>
> . . . I have big news to write. Jason has shot two Deers, one large one with a lovely head. He has sent the head off to have it set up. Your father says he has seen lots of Deers heads, but that is the best one he ever saw. Jason wants you to have some of the meat.
> . . . Jason got one last Friday, & this morning he got up at four o'clock and started out. Now he has come with his second Deer. I never see how excited he was. When he shot his first one, he was over the other side of the mountain, all alone, & he run all the way to the house to get help to get him to the house. Stant and Elmer [my grandfather's uncles] went & helped him. I felt glad for him. He wanted to get a deer so bad. Elmer has shot two deer, so he nor Jason can't shoot any more this year. . . .
>
> From Mother

"I shot those two bucks in just a day and a half of hunting," my grandfather told me. I could tell by his voice and manner that he was still proud of it to that day. You always remember your first deer, and in a family that hunts, everyone makes a

Family photograph

Jason Bennett, age 16, with one of the two deer that he shot. c. 1906.

big thing of it. Back in my grandfather's day, when farms were
largely self-sustaining, bringing in a deer was often greeted
with great celebration. To Elvira and Ransom's family, it meant
fresh venison, which was a great delicacy. The heart, liver, and
tenderloin were among the first meals served up.

If it had been cold enough, the deer could have been left
to hang, but the day my grandfather shot his second deer,
the temperature rose to 60 degrees, and stayed above freezing that night. Under those conditions, a deer couldn't be left
hanging too long, but the meat could be kept in iceboxes if it
was used up in a short time. In 1906, there were no refrigera-
tors at Elvira and Ransom's farm; electricity wouldn't come
to the area for decades. Meat was often preserved by salting,
smoking, and canning, these methods allowing most of a deer
to be consumed for food.

My grandfather had the deer head that had so impressed
his grandfather mounted. The taxidermist was J. Waldo Nash
in nearby Norway, at the time one of the state's seventeen
licensed taxidermists. That deer's head hung over my grandfather's desk all the years he was alive, and I had admired it as a
boy, despite the cracks that had appeared. It also had another
effect on me in my boyhood years.

That deer head led me to venture into taxidermy, with all
the youthful excitement and imagination a young boy could
have. I became a devoted student of Professor J. W. Elwood,
BS, president of the Northwestern School of Taxidermy. I
knew that this school was highly regarded because it was
advertised for years in *Popular Mechanics*, my favorite magazine
when I was a boy. The school's course of study was described

as a "Comprehensive Treatise on Collecting and Preserving All Subjects of Natural History."

I had spent months wishing that I could enroll, and remember my excitement when I finally ordered the lessons. The wait seemed endless. Ideas about animals I wanted to mount washed over me in waves of anticipation. The course came in the form of nine pamphlet-size books containing forty lessons in all. It covered collecting, killing, skinning, and mounting birds; skinning and mounting small and large animals, game heads, fish, eels, sharks, snakes, frogs, turtles, and alligators; novelty taxidermy; craft work; tanning; and other miscellaneous information, like how to deal with open mouths, tongues, feet, bats, removing skunk odor, repairing broken fish fins, and a plethora of other extremely useful, practical, and exciting information.

Of course, I had also ordered the recommended tools and materials from the equally highly regarded J. W. Elwood Supply Co., Inc. These included a brain spoon, scalpel, bone scraper, snips, forceps, cartilage knife, saw, tape measure, brush, and scissors. I also purchased a variety of glass eyes, which were specially manufactured in the revered Elwood's Glass Eye Factory, as well as wire of various gauges to support specimens, preservative (borax), a ball of cotton twine, excelsior (shredded wood), linen thread and needles, potter's clay, cotton, pins, artist's brushes and oil paints, and soft shredded hemp, called *tow*, for building small bird bodies.

Professor Elwood informed me in Lesson One that I was about to learn an art second only to painting and sculpturing. He urged me to read the entire contents of Book One before starting. "Every sentence means something," he pointed out,

"and deserves your most careful attention and consideration."
Professor Elwood was all business. Lesson Two instructed me
on the collecting and fine art of killing my first specimen,
preferably a small bird killed by a shotgun using fine-size shot.
And so I was launched into a different world of nature study.

Bowing to Professor Elwood's wise counsel, I chose a bird as
one of my first projects. Grandmother Abbott, on my mother's
side, had a birdfeeder by her back porch in the village of Bryant Pond, and she gave me permission to shoot a blue jay.
There were houses all around, but in those days, it wasn't all
that unusual to hear a gunshot outside your window. People
were always shooting woodchucks, crows, and other var-
mints, as they called them—a rich resource for J. W. Elwood's
curriculum.

So, using my father's .410 gauge shotgun, I positioned
myself inconspicuously on the back porch in such a way that
I could face the feeder and shoot away from nearby houses. A
blue jay flew in, and I downed it with my first shot—clean: no
holes in the ceiling, no splintered railing, no broken windows.

Professor Elwood's instructions were clear and detailed,
and I followed them carefully, mounting the blue jay on a
perch and making a nice wooden wall plaque. With a feeling
of accomplishment, I started to expand both my imagination
and my skills. I began mounting mammals. The first was a
gray squirrel: not so good. After a time, I tried another one, a
red squirrel this time: better. My best result came years later
when I mounted a bobcat head. I set the mouth open with
teeth bared, inserted a carved wooden tongue, and molded
the whole interior with colored wax until it seemed realistic to
me. But to another bobcat? I was never sure.

Of course, I'm aware that taxidermy has both proponents and opponents today. There are those who see it as another troubling example of viewing nonhuman animals as objects of lesser importance, an opinion that is disrespectful of their rights as valuable cohabitants of his planet. There are others who view taxidermy as having some scientific and educational value, to which many museum exhibits attest. Still others view it as an art form, which promotes an aesthetic appreciation of wildlife. I learned recently that mounted animals have a new role in interior design as a way to add interest, richness, and beauty to commercial establishments and residences.[1]

Back in 1906, my grandfather sold the hides of his two deer to one of the 122 licensed dealers of deerskins in the state. Leather from deerskin has a long history as a valuable commodity, which goes back to its use by Native Americans who populated this country when it was first colonized by Europeans. Deerskin leather is still popular for gloves, footwear, and other clothing. It is unusually soft and supple, as well as strong, stretchable, and breathable. However, it is not naturally water- and stain-resistant, and can lose its shape.

Deer hunting in 1906 was also a big business in the state for other reasons. Maine had 137 proprietors of hunting camps, and 76 market men who were licensed to buy and sell deer meat to local customers. There were 2,083 guides registered that year, producing an estimated income of $360,000 for the season. Although my grandfather wasn't required to have a license, 1906 was the first year that nonresidents were required to buy one, at a cost of $15 apiece. This brought in about $31,500 to the State from 2,100 out-of-state hunters.[2]

My grandfather's two deer were among an estimated 18,000 deer taken in Maine that year, as reported by the commissioners of Inland Fisheries and Game. Although it seems like a lot, it was actually a marked decline when compared with the previous year—fully one-third less. And beyond their estimate of 18,000 deer killed, the commissioners figured that a full one-third more were killed for which they had no record, including poaching by some operators of sporting and logging camps, and by "so-called" fishermen, canoeing parties, and campers, who were in the woods with guns, spring, summer, and fall. The commissioners concluded that "drastic measures must be instituted" to prevent such illegal hunting activity.[3]

My grandfather wasn't thinking about the commissioners' worries, however; his successful shooting of his first (and second) deer was the high point of that year on his grandfather's farm, and it contributed much to the good feelings he carried for the rest of his life about his experience working there. Among them was a love for this country around Shadagee, and by the end of the year, the seeds of his desire to own a piece of it had been planted.

CHAPTER TWO

Shadagee

*Jason, Donald, and Dean were over in the woods in back of the Old
Cellar . . .*
—SEPTEMBER 7, 1942, CAMP SHEEPSKIN REGISTER

E levated sixteen feet above the ground and surrounded
by woods, I'm in the dooryard of E. Swan, at least
according to the 1858 map of Greenwood, Maine. "E"
probably stands for Edmund, which I'd once seen on a deed to
this lot dated April 27, 1875, with the name Edmund N. Swan
on it. All that remains of E. Swan's home are neatly placed
rocks, which form the granite foundation of his farmhouse. As
long as I can remember, my family has called it the Old Cellar.
It's one of many remnants of farms in the woods all over this
country where my hunting stand is located. Some are those of
my ancestors, echoing a long tradition of living off the land
here, and Ransom Cole wasn't the first.

Ransom Cole was the third generation to have a farm
in Shadagee, better known as Greenwood Center, for its

geographic location in the middle of the town of Greenwood. The name *Shadagee* is a curious designation. Historical researcher and teacher Larry Glatz suggests the name
may have come from local veterans of the War of 1812, who
fought in a dense hemlock swamp in the valley of the Chateauguay River in Canada, just west of Lake Champlain. The
battle plans went awry when the men became lost and were
forced to retreat.

After the war, the soldiers returned home to settle in the
remote, forested area surrounding Ransom's farm. Glatz con-
jectures that this heavily wooded locality may have reminded
them of the Chateauguay woods, and, not being familiar with
French, they corrupted the name *Chateauguay* to Shadagee
(with a hard "g," as in "gear").[1] Today, Shadagee is a settlement of homes and cottages in an area on the west side of
Twitchell Pond along the Greenwood Road, between a line of
mountains and the shore of the pond.

One who would have well understood the connection made
by the veterans of the Battle of the Chateauguay between the
river region in Canada and Shadagee was Ransom's grandfather, Calvin Cole Sr. An early settler in Shadagee, Calvin
acquired a deed in 1832 to a tract of wild land.[2] He was soon
followed by four sons, one being Elbridge, who continued
the family tradition of tilling the soil. One of Elbridge and
Arabelle Cole's eleven children was Ransom, born in 1842.[3]
Eleven children is a large family by any standard. The average
family in 1850 in the United States was six to seven people.
Limited birth control played a role in producing large families
at that time, but another contributing factor was the need for
labor in families that farmed and ran mills.

Photograph courtesy of the Greenwood Historical Society

Ransom and Elvira Cole (at left) with three of their children on their
Shadagee farm, c. 1887.

As soon as Ransom was big enough, he was initiated by his
father into the agricultural life on the family farm. As a young
man, he began to farm on his own, and subsequently became
a prominent businessman. He owned the 900-acre farm my
grandfather would work on for two years, overseeing its
diverse operations of dairying; raising cattle, sheep, and crops;
and running a sawmill, manufacturing lumber of all kinds. He
married Elvira Cole in 1863, a widow with three living sons.
She had seven more children by Ransom, including my great-
grandmother Mary. Ransom's farm is still in the Cole family,
and deer and hunting still excite people who live in this area.

A lot of undeveloped hunting country still remains in the
Shadagee area today, and it isn't strolling land. It's up and

Photograph by the author

Rowe's Ledge looking north. Twitchell Pond is in the foreground and a part of Shadagee is on the far shore on the top left side of the photo.

down—steep and high in places, with mountains and knolls, interspersed with ponds and lowland swamps and bogs. To get over Tibbetts Mountain, located behind Ransom's farm, and where he shot his first deer in 1906, my grandfather had to climb more than 700 feet above the farm, up steep, heavily wooded, rocky land—typical terrain for this region in the foothills of the White Mountains.

My grandfather didn't know it at the time, but that mountain and the difficulties it gave him that day were directly related to massive land movement that had occurred hundreds of millions of years ago. A glacier bulldozed its way over this rough country, moving from the northwest to the southeast between 25,000 and 18,000 years ago, comparatively recent when measuring the passage of geologic time. The result was a shaping of mountains and ridges, leaving many of them with slopes on their northwest sides that gradually rose to bluffs and ledges at their south or southeast ends, and a landscape strewn with rocks and boulders.

My grandfather couldn't have helped but notice the shiny flakes of mica in some of the exposed ledges, clues to one of the United States' largest concentrations of semiprecious minerals—quartz, beryl, tourmaline, and many others—that was discovered years later in this region. The area is now pocked, like Swiss cheese, with holes from old mine excavations. Just a few miles south of where he hunted, the Tiger Bill Quarries gouge out a mountain's bedrock. Here, a deposit of pegmatite, a coarse-grained igneous rock, was initially explored in the 1930s, nearly three decades after my grandfather dragged his deer over this rocky country. Today, hunters in this hilly land will occasionally find themselves on an old mine road instead of a logging road.

The rocky soils, climate, and hilly character of this country made farming difficult, but it produced beautiful, mixed-hardwood forests of red oak, beech, white and yellow birch, and sugar and red maple, along with stands of white pine, hemlock, spruce, and white cedar. It's not surprising that the enterprising nature of Ransom Cole led him to expand his business beyond farming to include a sawmill at the outlet of Twitchell Pond, where a dam provided a dependable supply of waterpower.

These enterprises and hunting deer kept my grandfather busy that fall of 1906, and they were not unrelated. He knew that deer were attracted to the fields of the farm, and that the hardwood trees processed in the sawmill produced food crops of beechnuts and acorns that deer sought out every fall, leaving ruffled trails in deep layers of pawed leaves covering the ground in the surrounding forests. On that day of November 19, 1906, he may well have known about a good stand of beech or oak on the other side of Tibbetts Mountain that seemed to him a promising place to hunt. Whatever his motivation, it paid off with a deer—not a foregone conclusion when one hunts an animal so wily and smart.

If my grandfather had read the previous month's issue of *The Maine Sportsman*, a widely circulated monthly journal, any notions he may have had about the cleverness of deer would have been reinforced. The publication contained a piece by Ernest Thompson Seton reprinted from *Scribner's Magazine*. It offered valuable insight into the white-tailed deer's mind:

> By reason of its singular adaptability and gifts, it is the only one of our deer that can live contentedly and unsuspectedly in 100 acres of thicket. It is the only one that can sit unconcernedly all the day long while factory whistles and bells are sounding around it and yet distinguish at once the sinister twig snap that tells of some prowling foe as far away, perhaps, as the other noises.
>
> It is the only one that, hearing a hostile footfall, will sneak around to find the cause, study the trail, and then glide, catlike, through the brush to a farther haven, without even trying to see the foe or give him a chance for a shot. It is the least migratory, the least polygamous, the least roving, as well as the swiftest,

keenest, shyest, wisest, most prolific, and most successful of our deer. . . .[4]

There was no way that my grandfather could have known
it at the time, but one day he would become aware of such
a deer—a creature that would not only frequent the swamp
where he hunted, but would haunt him for the rest of his life.

CHAPTER THREE

Deer Herd

. . . we went hunting but all we saw was each other.
—NOVEMBER 11, 1938, CAMP SHEEPSKIN REGISTER

I t's been shooting time for nearly a half-hour now, and I haven't heard another shot anywhere. It's too quiet for opening day. Some years, I'd have heard half a dozen shots by now. I hope it's not a sign of what the hunting situation might be like this year—how many deer there might be around. We had kept a sharp eye out for tracks while putting up the stands the day before, and had seen a few, but it takes a little snow to see them well with so many leaves on the ground. On the other hand, sitting in a stand with crisp, frozen leaves on the ground below makes it easier to hear something coming, especially when you've taken your hearing aids out.

Every fall, the elusive nature of deer was not the only subject discussed around woodstoves throughout Maine, until the embers died or someone fell asleep. There were other topics that received much speculation beyond the frequent futility, even occasional embarrassment, of trying to match wits with a deer. One that always seemed to dominate the talk was the fluctuation of the deer herd, and it was carried beyond the warmth of the stove, sometimes with great optimism.

During October 1906, my grandfather might well have seen the item in the locally distributed newspaper, the *Oxford Democrat*, which said: "If hunters have any kind of luck, there should be a stack of game coming out of the woods in the next few weeks. The hunters are going into the woods by the scores."[1] The news item referred to hunters, particularly those from out of state, stopping in Bangor to stock up for their hunting trips into the big woods to the north.

The month he got his two deer the mood changed, and my grandfather would have felt lucky to have gotten even one deer if he had followed reports on the health of the deer herd. *The Maine Sportsman* editorialized under the title "Is the Deer Supply Decreasing?" about the recent "astonishing falling off" of railroad shipments of large, hunter-killed game animals compared to the previous year."[2]

The fluctuation of the deer population in the Greenwood area had been a common occurrence during the years leading up to my grandfather's success. A view of this in the mid-1800s was given by a man with an unusual background for one born in Greenwood. Addison Emery Verrill was born in 1839, three years before Ransom Cole and five miles away, but he grew to see deer and other wildlife from an entirely different perspective, having educational advantages that Ransom did not have.

Verrill graduated from Harvard in 1864, after training under the legendary scientist Louis Agassiz, and became professor of zoology at Yale. In a series of articles, "Recollections of Early Settlers of Greenwood," which he wrote for the *Oxford County Advertiser* in the early 1900s, he described not only the settlers in Greenwood, including my ancestors, but also the country and its wildlife. He noted that in his boyhood, which would have been in the 1840s and early '50s, deer were never seen, nor were wolves, but in recent times (early 1900s), he said that deer had become common. He speculated that they probably had migrated from northern New York, Vermont, and New Hampshire, and were followed by wolves.[3]

Verrill's articles were published in the local paper in 1914, when my grandfather was twenty-four, so he probably read them with interest. It wouldn't be until he reached his seventies, however, near the end of his hunting days, that he would have had an opportunity to read an especially insightful perspective on the deer situation before and after his 1906 hunting success. It was in a booklet on the history of the white-tailed deer in Maine, written by Don C. Stanton and published in 1963.[4]

Stanton corroborated Verrill's observations about the absence of both wolves and deer. He pointed out that in the 1840s and '50s the deer herd had headed downward in numbers, leading to a large die-off that occurred between 1864 and 1865. By 1880, the deer population was in a steep climb upward, peaking in 1895, then dipping to a low in 1906, and continuing to fluctuate. During those years between 1880 and 1920, Stanton noted that Maine experienced a period of many changes in the state's deer population, along with the factors that affected it.[5]

Stanton further observed something that my grandfather knew well: The interspersion of farmlands and woodlands "become some of the finest of deer range."[6] Deer thrive in a patterned landscape of edges, where farmlands of hayfields, pastures, croplands, and orchards meet woodlands of swamps, riparian areas, bogs, and forests of varied ages. Such a landscape provides a rich mix of food and cover, and was already in evidence when European explorers and settlers first encountered the Native American villages in New England. As the Europeans began clearing the land for farms, the deer population expanded. But too much clearing in some areas, such as in southern Maine, resulted in the loss of favorable habitat, and with that, a decline in deer numbers.[7] In 1880, ten years before my grandfather was born, Maine reached its peak of land clearing for farming, but by the time my grandfather was hunting in Shadagee, farmlands in the state were decreasing and reverting back to woodlands.[8] This change in areas where farming had been a predominant use of the land initially improved the habitat for deer.

In the hilly country of western Maine, farmland varied greatly in topography, soils, size, and configuration. I saw this firsthand. As a boy, my major means of transportation was a bicycle. This allowed me to take summer jobs picking beans and weeding corn in nearby East Bethel. The cornfields were located on large expanses of flat floodplain, rich soil that bordered the Androscoggin River, while the bean crops were inland, two miles. In just that short distance, the farms had changed to small, sloped fields nestled among steep ridges and hills. Here, the land was marginal for farming, being rocky, steep, and nutrient-poor. Such was the case for Shadagee and many other locations in western Maine towns, where farms were relatively small and surrounded by woods. The result was an edge effect of borderlands around the farms, which was always prevalent after the first farms were carved out of the wilderness. This characteristic of the local farmlands did not go unnoticed by my grandfather and the other hunters of that time, who made it a practice to observe where deer tended to congregate.

My grandfather also observed something else that had an effect on the deer herd in his area: wood harvesting. Throughout the early years of my grandfather's life, in the 1890s and early 1900s, the practice of harvesting big white pines and other old-growth trees for logs as the principal wood product was ending, and there was less "cut out and get out" logging, as Stanton termed it. Hardwood logs of maple, birch, ash, and other species were increasingly being hauled off the mountains surrounding Shadagee and other places in western Maine for use in the wood-turning mills, where many of my ancestors worked, including my grandfather's father, Frank Bennett; my grandfather and grandmother, from time to time; my father and mother; and my other grandfather, Leslie Abbott, my mother's father.

These mills included the E. L. Tebbetts Spool Company in Locke's Mills; the L. M. Mann and Sons clothespin factory and Captain John Dearborn's spool mill in Bryant Pond; a spool stock and dowel mill in Bethel; and C. B. Cummings & Son Company, which had produced dowels and other wood products since 1860, and the Tubbs Snowshoe Company, which

Photograph courtesy of the Greenwood Historical Society

Lumber yard at spool mill, c. 1890. The effect of wood harvesting on the changing landscape also affected its wildlife. In the distance, the row of homes along lower Main Street of Locke's Mills includes the homes of Jason Bennett and the author, 2nd and 3rd from the left.

started up in 1906 making ash snowshoes, skis, sleds, and furniture, both located in Norway, Maine.

Hardwood trees weren't the only ones being heavily cut in the late 1800s and early 1900s. Statewide, Maine was experiencing a great demand for softwood trees by the rapidly growing pulp and paper industry, with such mills as the Oxford Paper Company in nearby Rumford, fifteen miles away from Shadagee, which had begun operation around the beginning of the century. The pulp mills at that time were using hemlock, spruce, and balsam fir, the dark growth my grandfather talked about, found on the tops of mountains, in lowland areas, and in small pockets, such as ravines and small valleys, scattered across the rough western Maine landscape. Because this region produced more pine and hardwoods than spruce and fir, Stanton pointed out that the pulp cutters and paper mills were more attracted to northern and eastern Maine, where those two softwood species were more plentiful.[9]

In Maine, softwood production peaked in 1907, and hardwood in 1909.[10] Although early forest harvesters found clearcutting more economical—a practice that often wiped out deer yards and interrupted a steady supply of deer food—this kind of cutting operation became less widespread than in the previous century. In Greenwood, the woodlots were small compared to those being consolidated in the north woods. Cutting in the town covered the whole array of practices, from thinning to clear-cutting, depending on whether the wood was to be used for firewood, construction lumber, paper pulp, spool stock, and so on. The countryside took on the appearance of a patchwork of forests, some thinned, some clear-cut, and some untouched for years.

My grandfather not only saw all of this firsthand, he was also a part of it. At the age of nine, he was hauling logs down steep wood roads with a team of horses in the winter, off the very mountains he would be hunting years later behind Ransom's farm. This was a dangerous job for anyone, but this experience gave him an opportunity to observe deer coming into the cuts in winter to get at the tops left in slash piles. He also learned that the cutting of deer yards had a serious effect on deer survival in winter.

The severity of the winters also had a devastating impact on deer populations. The commissioners' report of 1905, for example, indicated a marked decline in the deer population after two harsh winters in 1903 and 1904, which resulted in a shortage of food.[11] In a letter published in the December 1906 issue of *The Maine Sportsman*, a hunter noted that the previous winter, "thousands of deer perished because they could not reach their feed [cedar tips and spills] in the swamps."[12]

The problem of deer survival in winter is still of great concern today among game managers, biologists, hunters, and the general public. We now know much more about the mortality of deer in winter and the importance of deer wintering areas, their characteristics, and why we need to protect and manage them to help deer survive severe winters.[13] This concern and knowledge has produced guidelines for protecting deer

Photograph by the author

A deer yard in winter.

wintering areas, along with a wealth of research on the effectiveness of state regulations aimed at protecting the wintering deer herd.[14]

Interestingly, in the long run, climate change might help to ease the wintering problems of deer and push their natural range northward. Moose in Maine, on the other hand, are highly vulnerable to climate change, and their populations will likely diminish with higher temperatures.[15]

Back in my grandfather's youth at the turn of the twentieth century, climate change, as seen today, was rarely thought about, if at all; however, it was a time when forest conservation was just beginning to creep into forest management practices. This was spurred on by the growing number of large corporate land and mill owners, who needed to manage the forests wisely in order to ensure a dependable supply of wood. To do this, they needed trained foresters who would apply scientific forestry to cut more sustainably.

These foresters were also aware of the needs of wildlife, and through the years they have worked increasingly with game managers to protect the deer herd. Managing the habitat of deer was only one concern for the state after forming a game management agency; deer predation was another. The big predators, the wolf and mountain lion, are no longer factors, due in part to hunting and trapping, but predation is a natural function in nature and is still with us today, as are the issues and debates surrounding it with regard to preserving the deer herd.

CHAPTER FOUR

Predators

Coming back to camp . . . it looked like a panther . . .
— MAY 15, 1974, CAMP SHEEPSKIN REGISTER

I t's so quiet this morning that the loudest sound is the stillness. Then I jump, and a shiver runs up my spine. A loud
chorus of yips, barks, and howls comes out of the swamp
over beyond the Old Cellar, reaches a crescendo, dies down,
and absolute silence returns. Not another sound do I hear. I
know what it was: a pack of coyotes. We started hearing them
here in the 1970s. My grandfather never heard them; they
moved into these parts right after he'd left this planet. The
wolf they replaced had left before he arrived, but there was
another predator that seemed to stay around, and that was the
mountain lion.

Addison Verrill said that "the cougar or catamount was
sometimes, though very rarely, seen in Greenwood in the days
of the first settlers, but its hideous wailing cry was not infre-
quently heard."[1]

31

Composite photograph created by the author

Mountain lion and deer.

When my grandfather worked in Shadagee in 1906, it was likely that he didn't think much about mountain lions, but he probably had heard stories about them. Two incidences had occurred in the Shadagee area in the late 1800s that were still in the recollections of at least a few of the town's residents. It was in the late 1870s that a boy, George Clinton Cole Jr., was walking on the Greenwood Road to his home near Shadagee after selling his mother's butter in nearby Locke's Mills. It was dusk when he reached the shore of South Pond near his home. According to local historian, Blaine Mills: "Suddenly, young George realized that a very large mountain lion was stalking him in the bushes along the road. The cat continued to follow George for some distance. The boy was scared out of his wits and started to sing as loud as he could. Eventually, the cat disappeared, but the incident left the boy badly shaken. His next trip to Locke's Mills was unnerving, but the cat never reappeared."[2]

A little over a decade later, in 1891, the year after my grandfather was born, the Greenwood column in a local newspaper conveyed the following about another encounter with a mountain lion in Shadagee, less than two miles from where my grandfather had shot his deer:

> One evening last week Sylvester Cole was returning home from his work in the mill. He was about half a mile from his home when he noticed something coming towards him. In the twilight, he thought it was his dog coming to meet him, but soon realized it belonged to the feline tribe, and a large one at that.
>
> The animal approached within about ten feet of Mr. Cole and crouched as if it intended to spring on him. Sylvester started to take steps backward, looking for a stick or club. Unable to find any defensive weapon, he reached a small sapling tree and climbed as high as he could. The animal now had Sylvester treed only about five feet off the ground. Soon the cat was nearly under the tree and appeared about ready to spring onto Mr. Cole, so he started to holler for assistance. His family

finally heard him hollering and came to the rescue
with the dog and lantern. The animal leisurely strolled
off into the woods.

Mr. Cole described the beast as the size of a sheep,
somewhat shaggy with dull yellow fur. It had a short
round head, with bright glittering eyes and small ears.
Mr. Cole said it closely resembled a small lion. He has
no idea as to what kind of animal it was. It acted men-
acingly, but never made a sound.[3]

My grandfather, like most hunters, was always interested in
stories like these, for hunters are always curious about what
the woods hide, like those who fish are intrigued about what
lies beneath the surface of the water. This is especially true
when an incident occurs near to their hunting territory during
the years they are hunting it.

Such was the case in 1947 when a report came from the
old Sylvester Cole place, the same Sylvester Cole who had
scrambled into a tree to escape the lion. The land and Sylvester's old farmhouse had come into the ownership of Herb and
Ruby Mason of Locke's Mills, who were staying there during
summer vacations and weekends. Herb was known by everyone in town because every spring, he came by with a team of
horses and a wagon that he would back up to everyone's outhouse, removing a year's worth of human waste—yesterday's
equivalent to today's septic tank service.

Herb's encounter was described by Blaine Mills:

Herb was down in the lower field mowing with
a hand scythe when he felt the hair stand up on the

back of his neck. He turned around and there was the
largest cat he had ever seen crouched in the tall grass.
He told me he thought the cat was sizing him up, but
it never made a sound. Herb hollered several times
for Ruby to bring his rifle, but being hard of hearing,
she just kept saying, "What?" The cat finally got tired
of the game and strolled off through the hayfield and
into the woods.[4]

The next year, my father heard about another incident that
took place even closer to our camp, during the November
hunting season. The information had come from Dwight
Martin, who worked at the same wood-turning mill where my
father worked. Dwight was a Shadagee resident who lived
across Twitchell Pond from the camp. Blaine Mills recounted
the story many years later:

Dwight had shot a deer [earlier] in November. He
had nailed the deer hide to the woodshed door. The-
resa [his wife] was approaching the back door with
a basket of laundry to hang on the clothesline. On
passing the last window she saw a large mountain lion
sniffing the deer hide. She called her husband at work
in Locke's Mills, but the cat was long gone before he
arrived home.[5]

My father didn't say much about the mountain lion at the
time, but years later he had his own encounter at our camp. It
was in the spring of 1974. He had walked down the Sheepskin
Bog Road from Mont Brooks's farm at the top of Rowe Hill,
the road being too muddy to drive beyond that point. He

had a shovel with him for cleaning out the ditched turnouts that drain water away from the road. He wrote in the camp register:

> I arrived at camp about 8:45 a.m. I went for a walk after I arrived to see if there were any deer left. I saw where one was running at the corner. Coming back to camp I saw an animal going by the toilet; it was as big as a good-size dog, but it was not a coy dog [a cross between a coyote and a domestic dog]. I only saw it a very few seconds (perhaps three). I believe it had short hair and a long tail, and the nose was not like a police dog's; in fact, it looked like a panther, but expect that everybody would say I was telling a big story if I said so. It did not make any noise. I have been wondering if that animal was making the noise when Elsie and I was down there April 20–21.
>
> —Donald W. Bennett

Whatever it was, it was never seen again around the camp area, and it now shares a place in our minds whenever we speculate on the mysteries of these Sheepskin woods.

The eastern cougar was placed on the list of Endangered and Threatened Wildlife by the US Fish and Wildlife Service (USFWS) in 1975, and is protected under the act in twenty-one states, including Maine. In 2014 the USFWS began a review to determine the status of the eastern cougar in the East, especially to assess if it is truly extirpated in the region. It is the first review since the agency published a recovery plan for the cougar in 1982.[6]

Eastern Timber Wolf.

Another large predator of deer, long extirpated from Maine, is the eastern timber wolf, *Canis lupus lycaon*. In Colonial times, the wolf was relentlessly subjected to extermination efforts. In Maine a statewide bounty was placed on the animal in 1832, remaining in effect until 1916. In Farmington, some thirty miles from Camp Sheepskin, the last wolf recorded in that town met its end around 1844.[7] By 1960, the wolf was apparently gone from Maine.

The existence of the wolf in the state is still debated. While wildlife experts agree that Maine has abundant wolf habitat, there appears to be no documentation of a breeding population. Like the mountain lion, however, reports of sightings and other evidence—such as seeing tracks and scat and hearing howls—of its existence in Maine have continued through the years, to present day.

A century after the extirpation of the wolf from Maine, another canine predator of deer, the coyote, was considered to be already well established in western and central Maine. At Camp Sheepskin, we were increasingly becoming aware of its presence in our hunting area. Maine's coyote population resulted from the species' gradual dispersal from the Midwest. One was trapped in the state around the time the camp was built in the mid-1930s. By the 1960s, an increase was noticed in the western parts of the state. In 1999, between 300 and 400 coyotes were estimated to be living in the wildlife management district in which our camp is located.[8]

The earliest note in our camp register about coyotes was my father's mention of a coydog, a hybrid between a coyote and a dog, when he thought he had seen a mountain lion. During the decade of the 1990s, we recorded more evidence of the presence of coyotes. On November 11, 1993, our hunting party "heard a coyote pack howling." Two years later, on November 7, 1995, I saw a coyote one early morning as I approached my stand up behind our camp. In March of 1997, my son Rick and his wife Karen spent a couple of days cross-country skiing at camp and saw coyote tracks between the Old Cellar and the Hall's Ridge behind Sheepskin Bog. That November my son-in-law Chuck Martin saw a coyote from his stand near Tracy Mountain. In 1998, my daughter Cheryl, sitting in her stand one early morning, heard coyotes howling—first, near Jason's Mountain, and then, near Tracy Mountain. Later in the season, we discovered that a dead coyote had been thrown over the bank at the edge of the bog at the camp turn by the Sheepskin Bog Road.

There is ample evidence that coyotes will prey on deer. Two times in my life I've seen coyotes after deer. The first was in early March of 1992. My wife Sheila and I had skied down the side of Chase Rapids along the Allagash River so that I could photograph the river during winter for a book I was work- ing on. While I was taking photos, directly across the river from us a large male coyote began to stalk a deer that had just crossed the river upstream. The deer saw the coyote, and it bounded along the riverbank with the predator in hot pursuit. I photographed the whole episode as the deer made good its getaway by jumping into the river and coming back onto our side.

My second experience occurred a few years ago at our home in Mount Vernon one August day. Sheila and I were having our morning coffee on our back porch, overlooking our field. A large coyote appeared and began foraging in the field for blueberries. We had watched it for some time when a fawn came into the field in front of us, some distance from the coyote. At first the coyote didn't see the fawn. Then it caught sight of it and instantly flattened itself to the ground and watched. Suddenly the coyote lunged forward and raced toward the little deer, leaping onto it, taking it by the throat, and pulling it to the ground. It was all over within seconds; a few minutes later, the coyote had dragged the deer out of the field and into the woods.

How to treat predators of deer has been the subject of intense debate among sportsmen, scientists, and others, including the public at large. There are those who say that cougars, wolves, and coyotes should be eliminated. Let the deer hunters manage the herd. The funds from the licenses they purchase can be used to help the State manage not only the deer, but an array of game and nongame species. There are those who say that these predators are desirable for balanced, diverse, and healthy-functioning ecosystems, and that wolves and cougars should at least be encouraged to reestablish themselves in Maine's ecosystems, if not outright reintroduced. At this writing there is no closed season on hunting coyotes with firearms during daylight hours, except on Sundays. Other laws also apply to coyote hunting and trapping.

Among all of the elements that kill deer, the one that concerns me most is chronic wasting disease (CWD). This is a fatal disease of the deer's nervous system, along with other members of its family, including moose. This ailment belongs to a family of diseases that includes mad cow disease in cattle. It has been found in deer in a number of states, including New York, which is closest to Maine. The disease is monitored by Maine every year, but to date, no evidence of its presence has been detected. There is also no evidence that CWD can infect humans. An infected deer herd would have catastrophic consequences on the hunting of white-tails in this state. To prevent the introduction of CWD in Maine, in addition to monitoring for the disease, the Department of Inland Fisheries and Wildlife is keeping the public informed, and working with other agencies in this state and other states, along with the federal government and private organizations.[9]

From a historical perspective, the greatest influence on the deer population in Maine and elsewhere is the human animal. In Greenwood, as in other places, this influence began when a means of transportation opened up wild areas for settlement, forest harvesting, farming, and hunting. For inland areas such as Shadagee, these activities were dependent on roads.

CHAPTER FIVE

Deer Town

Finished short path to county road.
—OCTOBER 2, 1937, CAMP SHEEPSKIN REGISTER

I hear a vehicle coming down Rowe Hill on the Sheepskin
Bog Road, across the bog from me—most likely a hunter
at this time of day. It slows down at the bottom of the hill,
but then I hear it going along the edge of the bog on the Old
County Road, toward the lower end of the wetlands. This is
somewhat unusual, because most people going that way park
at the turnaround at the bottom of the hill by our camp turn
and then walk down the road. The Old County Road is now
impassable by cars and trucks beyond the bog. Beavers have
flooded the road, and two bridges are now gone.

I listen intently. Soon I hear tires spinning and the engine
revving. It sounds like it's stuck.

The Old County Road was the first to provide access to this
land. From a hunting perspective, it connected people with
hunting areas through the center of the town. In a sense, it

made Greenwood a "deer town," and even today the road still connects the range where I hunt to the rest of the world.

The road was built in 1820 when Maine became a state, one of three connecting the towns of Norway and Greenwood. From Greenwood City, the road originally went over Rowe Hill, down to Shadagee, and then followed the west sides of South Pond and Round Pond into Locke's Mills, a distance of about six or seven miles. Sometime before 1844 the road was rerouted around Rowe Hill, keeping to flat terrain. It passed along the edge of Sheepskin Bog and followed the east shore of Twitchell Pond under Rowe's Ledge, one of those south-eastern bluffs in the region, to join up with the original road in Shadagee.

The Old County Road also connected both sides of my grandfather's family—the Coles in Shadagee and the Bennetts near Greenwood City. My grandfather's mother married Frank Jerome Bennett, whose grandfather, Noah, and great-grandfather, Francis, had farms a mile north of Greenwood City, just off the Old County Road, and only a mile from where my stand is today. Frank's father grew up on Noah's farm. All of these families rode their wagons and carriages over the Old County Road to travel between Greenwood City and Locke's Mills, which took them through Shadagee. Until 1849, the route took them by Sheepskin Bog and the future site of our camp. In that year, the first dam and sawmill were built at the outlet of Twitchell Pond, which raised the pond and flooded the Old County Road, making it impassable beneath Rowe's Ledge.

By 1858, a new road, the Greenwood Road, had opened between Shadagee and Greenwood City, which ran along the west side of Twitchell Pond. This road more directly

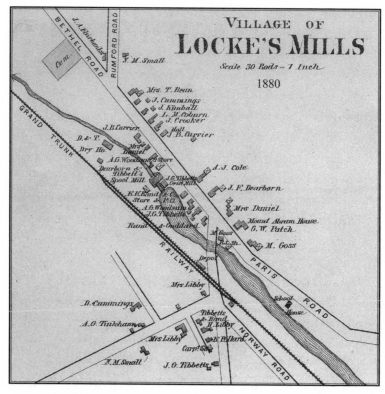

Published by Caldwell & Halfpenny, 1880

Village of Locke's Mills, Greenwood, Maine. Map from Oxford County, 1880, Maine. The Norway Road, in the bottom left corner of the map, led to the Old County Road in Shadagee.

connected the two settlements and my ancestors. In 1899, the Old County Road was discontinued from Sheepskin Bog by the east side of Twitchell Pond to Shadagee. This action set the stage for my family's emotional upheaval a hundred years later regarding our "hunting privileges."

My grandfather was nine years old when that section of the Old County Road was abandoned. He was born on October

13, 1890, in his grandfather Ransom Cole's weather-beaten yellow farmhouse. It was nine a.m., and his grandmother was just in the middle of the family wash. He would say in his later years, exhibiting the sense of humor for which he was known: "For the first two hours I lay there listening to the cows bellowing."

In his boyhood years, my grandfather's family moved around Greenwood and other towns in the area, depending on what jobs were available for his father. His father was an ox team-ster, working from daylight to dark hauling logs to one of the many hardwood turning mills and sawmills in the area. To stay employed, he also worked in lumber camps and in the mills.

When my grandfather was born, his family had a rental property in Bryant Pond. In his third year, the family moved to a house in Shadagee near his grandfather's birch mill. By the age of five, he was walking the one mile to school each day with his older brother, Willie (born Frank Willard). As soon as they had grown enough, he and Willie were expected to work to help keep the household going and the two were assigned a routine of chores. In his eighth year, when the family moved to a small farm near Shadagee, my grandfather drove cattle two miles to pasture every morning before school. After school he drove them back, watered and fed them, and cleaned out the stables. Every other night he walked two miles to the post office in Locke's Mills to pick up the mail.

When my grandfather was twelve, the family moved to a small farm just outside of Locke's Mills. By then he was in the eighth grade, and found a part-time job at the Mount Abram Hotel on Main Street in Locke's Mills. He took care of the stable, and in exchange for his work, he got room and board.

When he graduated from grammar school, he was financially unable to go to high school. This was a great disappointment to him, as he enjoyed school and had gotten good grades; so, instead of going to high school, he decided to go through the eighth grade again and, with his teacher's help, continue his education.

When his grammar school days were over, my grandfather continued to work for the hotel. In his thirteenth year, he worked in Portland for one of his uncles who owned a store in the city. After he returned to Locke's Mills, he got a job at the E. L. Tebbetts Spool Company mill, sanding and varnishing bobbins. After about three months, he was laid off because of lack of work, and spent the next year on his grandfather's farm in Shadagee—the year 1906 when he shot his first deer.

Sometime during my grandfather's teenage years, his father bought the Mount Abram Hotel. When my grandfather worked on Ransom Cole's farm, the hotel was my grandfather's recorded residence. The hotel was close to the train station, which made it a convenient place for vacationers to stay. In the fall season, the hotel's clientele included deer hunters, but by the time my grandfather's family lived there, the hotel had already established a connection with the hunting community—an unusual one that would influence hunting throughout the world in a way that could not have been imagined at that time.

The hotel had a long history of ownership. In 1873, after a major fire had destroyed the hotel, it was rebuilt by new proprietors, one of whom was Benjamin Bean, the father of Leon Leonwood Bean, who would become the famous founder of the L.L.Bean Company. Leon was born the year before, in

Photograph courtesy of the Greenwood Historical Society

"Good Hunting!" c. 1900-10. (L to R) Earnest Day, George Will Day, Herb Day—Gore Road near Greenwood town line.

1872, only a mile and a half from the hotel on Howe Hill, across the road from where the Mount Abram Skiway is now located. After the hotel had been rebuilt, the Bean family moved in. In 1877, Bean sold the hotel and moved from the town. Seven years later, in 1884, when young Leon was twelve, he lost both of his parents in a matter of days to illness.[1]

Leon was one of six orphaned children in the family. He lived with a family friend for the first year, then appears to have moved around, working and attending school in various places. At the age of thirteen or fourteen, he went on his first hunting trip with a cousin to Wild River Valley, near Gilead, Maine, about fifteen miles west of where he was born, in Greenwood. The first morning he shot his first deer. He returned the next year and shot a large buck. He was so taken by the Wild River country that he eventually leased the old office building of a logging camp and hunted out of it for more than thirty years.

When my grandfather's father moved his family into the hotel and it became his family's home, my grandfather shared the distinction of having lived in the same home that L. L. Bean once had. Later, in 1911, Leon invented his famous hunting shoe, leading to the establishment of his firm, L.L.Bean, known throughout the world. Today, L. L.'s boots still walk these hills every hunting season and sit next to the stove in our camp after every day's tramp.

In those early years, Locke's Mills was a thriving community. Main Street was also Route 26, a major highway that one could travel from coastal Portland into the mountains of New Hampshire via Grafton Notch and Upton, Maine. The village had many residences, a railroad station, a post office, several stores and shops, a school, a cemetery, and a church. Years later my grandfather liked to tell the story of how his uncle Elmer Cole once shot a deer and brought it to the church where townspeople were attending a meeting. Deer at the time were so scarce that when word got around, the meeting was stopped so that everyone could come out and look at it.

There was, however, another time in those early years when deer hunting caused a much bigger disruption of community normalcy, and it had to do with the mill.

The mill was the center of the village's economic activity. It had been built in 1819 by Samuel Locke Sr., to take advantage of the mixed hardwood forests on the surrounding hills and mountains, as well as the dependable supply of waterpower from the several ponds that drained into Alder River, flowing through the village. From that time on, a succession of mills has stood in the same location, despite being destroyed three times by fire. In 1851, the village was firmly established as the center of economic activity in the town of Greenwood, when the St. Lawrence & Atlantic Railroad bypassed Greenwood City and went through Locke's Mills.

In 1853, the railroad's name changed to the Grand Trunk Railroad, and connected Montreal and Portland. The railroad station in Locke's Mills was located in the center of the village near the mill. The railroad did a high volume of business during my grandfather's day, serving mills, farms, logging companies, and stores. In addition, it delivered mail, which was distributed through the local post office. In 1887, the railroad had three trains running from Montreal to Portland and three going the opposite direction, every day. Two carried passengers. When I was a boy, my parents didn't have an automobile, so whenever my mother wished to visit her parents and sister in Bryant Pond, four miles away, she would take me with her on a "down" train in the morning, and we would return on the "up" train in the afternoon. In 1960, this passenger train service ended.

While our lives in Locke's Mills were greatly influenced by the railroad, it was the mill upon which my family was dependent. The mill employed many of the town's residents—about 60 in 1900, and by 1932, about 150. Many of the workers lived within walking distance, timing their lives to the whistle, which blew at 6:50 a.m., to give a ten-minute warning; 7:00 a.m., when work started; 12:00 noon, when lunch break began; 12:50 p.m., another warning; 1:00 p.m., when work resumed; and 5:00 p.m., at the end of the work day. My grandfather and grandmother, as well as my father and mother

Photograph courtesy Greenwood Historical Society

Main Street, Locke's Mills, c. 1892, looking west. The spool mill is on the right and the post office where Jason Bennett, as a boy, picked up mail is at the bottom of the hill on the right.

in later years, all worked in the mill on this timetable. Today, those of us who grew up in Locke's Mills in the late 1930s and the '40s still remember the whistle and people walking from all directions to and from the mill on its schedule.

Some years the mill ran night shifts, depending on the amount of orders that were received. When it was operating, it was noisy for those living close by. There was a time when the mill ran on both waterpower and a large steam engine, the energy being transferred to saws and other machines by a huge system of wheels and belts that flapped and whined. For the workers inside, the air was filled with dust and a constant loud, rumbling din. The mill was the economic machine for the village and the surrounding area, providing a living for my grandfather's family and many others, and residents were fortunate to have it.

Yet there were times when a deep primal urge overcame the importance of the mill.

Sometime during the early years of the town's history, the owners decided the mill had to close on the opening day of deer hunting. The reason, quite simply, was the fact that no one showed up. So many workers were deer hunters, with no doubt in their minds that the best chance of shooting a deer was during the first days of the season, when the deer were unaware of the impending danger, and the herd had not yet been culled. And, of course, they also knew that there were always a few deer that were just plain foolish and would stumble out of the bush, startled and confused by all the shooting and hunters in the woods; they would just stand there, broadside, trying to fathom what was going on.

If the workers were lucky, it would all be over in just a few seconds, meaning they could return to work the next day, receiving all the accolades they deserved for being so skilled at hunting.

It wasn't just for deer hunting that the mill shut down; it was to meet the town's appetite for hunting in general. On October 25, 1892, a local newspaper reported in its Locke's Mills column that "the spool mill shut down Monday night and all hands went to a squirrel hunt Tuesday. The defeated side is to give an oyster supper the next Tuesday evening." A week later the column followed up: "The squirrel hunt supper last Tuesday evening was a grand success."[2]

There is no question that hunting held a special place in the town's way of life, and a great many of the town's residents viewed deer hunting as an essential activity in their lives. Townspeople would start discussing it well before the season arrived. Of course, few would give any specifics about where there were any deer. In fact, most people would readily say that there were *no* deer around, hoping to keep the competition down on opening day. But still, they would talk incessantly about guns, getting their camps ready, changes in the laws and regulations, and all the episodes of the past, just as if there were as many deer as ever. They would pore over advertisements for boots, clothing, and equipment in magazines, catalogs, and newspapers. Guides would gear up.

The Grand Trunk Railroad, through its extensive advertising network, would tout big-game hunting along its routes in an effort to lure hunters. Nonresident hunters would book into the Mount Abram Hotel. During the season, people would gather around the wagons carrying deer into town and comment on sizes and racks, listening with rapt attention to stories of the kills. People would stop by homes to see deer hung up, offer congratulations, and hear the tales that were told. It was in this environment that my grandfather, his children, and his grandchildren grew up, and many could hardly wait until they were old enough to carry a gun and hunt.

The excitement about hunting was reflected in the local newspapers that would carry stories and keep people informed of who had been successful. The Greenwood column in the *Oxford Democrat*, published in nearby South Paris, was always sprinkled with hunting news items through the October and November season, written by the paper's inquisitive, talented, and sometimes colorful reporter, Lemuel Dunham.

CHAPTER SIX

The Correspondent

Went to Dunham's house . . . asked them down to see the deer.
—NOVEMBER 20, 1943, CAMP SHEEPSKIN REGISTER

I t's light enough now so that I can see the big pines over where the old Dunham farmhouse once stood, on the other side of the Old County Road. Lemuel Dunham's great-grandson now has a small hunting camp over there. The farm's buildings have disappeared, and its orchard and fields have grown up, but the stories about deer hunting in this town, which were written in the Dunham farmhouse, are still with us. I know from them that in 1907, someone was waiting on the other side of the Old County Road not far from me for the same reason I am waiting today—for a deer to come by.

Lemuel Dunham was born in Hartford, Maine, in 1830. He grew up on a farm, and in his youth, he not only worked on the farm but also worked in an ax factory, went to sea and hauled cod and halibut on the Newfoundland Banks, and later, worked on a railroad.[3] Then, at the age of twenty-seven, he did something out of the ordinary: He enrolled in Hebron Academy in Hebron, Maine, to study English. Two years later he married a widow, Mrs. Lydia Clifford, and in 1875, after working a variety of jobs, he moved to a farmstead on Rowe Hill near Sheepskin Bog. He had bought the farm from George Bennett, the son of my grandfather's great-uncle, Daniel Bennett, a brother of Noah. Lemuel always referred to his farm as the Bennett place.

Lemuel and Lydia lived out the rest of their lives on Rowe Hill, raising a family along the way. Here, Lemuel labored on his farm, wrote poetry, explored his interests in the arts and sciences, and traveled throughout the town, making observations and gathering information for his weekly column in the *Oxford Democrat*. Following his death on October 4, 1915, the newspaper ran an item titled "A Valued Correspondent," praising his service to the newspaper and its readers. The paper remarked that "his removal is a distinct loss to those who for years have enjoyed the quaint and original local writings of 'L. D.' Here was a man who in a very limited local field had the ability to write of the little every-day happenings in such an entertaining way that . . . his locals were the leading feature of that department, and were complimented far and wide by the readers of the paper."[2]

One of the compliments came in a column from a nearby town, which was published on November 20, 1906, the day after my grandfather shot his second deer:

> Recently we much enjoyed a brief visit from your
> Greenwood correspondent, Mr. Lemuel Dunham. For
> a man who has seen over seventy-six years of active

life, he is remarkably active and retains his physical
and mental faculties well. Mr. Dunham is a reliable and
faithful recorder of the news of the day, and his correspondence for the *Democrat* would be much missed if
discontinued. He does not aspire to the flighty or sen-
sational, but aims to give true records of local events.
May he live to push the pencil for many years.[3]

True to form, Lemuel didn't neglect the reading public's
interest in deer hunting during that fall of 1906, when my
grandfather was a successful hunter. On October 16, with the
season well under way, he reported in his Greenwood column
that "our nimrod [skillful] hunter, Allon Cole, is out again with
an unknown companion, probably in pursuit of big game."[4] By
October 30, he was able to write that "only one deer has been
killed in town so as is known, Lester Morgan being the lucky
man. We took dinner with Sylvester Cole Sunday, and were so
fortunate as to get a taste of the meat and pronounced it fine."[5]
On November 20, two weeks after my grandfather had his
two deer, Lemuel reported that the deer hunting success had
picked up: "Home again," he wrote, "after a ramble of more
than two weeks, still 'this side up with care'—and here goes.
We rather expected to find some deer steak awaiting us on
reaching home, after those two falls of snow, and our expec-
tation was not disappointed. No less than nine deer have
been reported killed in town, and still the hunters are after
them." And in another item: "Ray, youngest son of J. A. Titus,
formerly of this town, went upcountry with several others
on a hunt and succeeded in getting a fine buck deer with ten
points. The others are reported as equally successful."[6]

As the season neared its end, Lemuel's column continued its news on the deer kill: "Last week the number of deer reported killed in this vicinity was nine, and now nearly as many more have been brought in. Last Saturday Walter Arkett of Bryant's Pond shot a fine buck and hauled him nearly two miles to the Bennett place [Lemuel's Rowe Hill farm], telephoned to the Pond for a team, and in about an hour was on his way home with his prize. That was the second one killed, and consequently, the last for season. Yes, the telephone is really a good thing to have; it saves divers steps and much valuable time."[7]

The last hunting item for the season was published on December 4: "Thursday morning . . . E. L. Dunham went out into an old orchard with his rifle, and getting into a favorable position waited for the result; in a short time along came a fine deer of about 200 pounds weight, and a moment later the animal lay struggling on the ground. We killed a pig only the day previous, and now he regrets the act on the ground of overproduction of fresh meat."[8]

The E. L. Dunham is Elton Dunham, Lemuel's son, born in 1873. In 1898, Lemuel arranged for the Rowe Hill farm to pass into his son's hands, with the understanding that he and Lydia would live and be cared for there, for the rest of their lives. By that time, Elton had married Mabel Morgan, my grandmother's sister. Lemuel lived at the farm until his death in 1915. The orchard where Elton got his deer that day remained productive for many years after the farm was abandoned, and it led to at least two big deer hunting disappointments that my grandfather experienced, one of them with me.

In the years following 1906 up until a year before his death, Lemuel reported faithfully on deer hunting in Greenwood.

During the 1907 hunting season, Lemuel wrote that "both big and small game are said to be scarce . . . , only three deer having been taken. . . ."[9]

A week later three incidents prompted Lemuel to report that "it would seem that big game is more plentiful of late than formerly." His grandson and a friend had "sighted a good-sized buck, and although they both fired several times at him, he was not hit in a vital spot. Though badly wounded and bleeding profusely, he made his escape as night came on, and they could no longer track him." They found the deer the next day "dead enough to skin." The second event Lemuel reported was his neighbor's success: "Dannie Bryant secured one of smaller size. . . ."

Photograph courtesy of the Greenwood Historical Society

Lemuel Dunham, 1830-1915, was a successful farmer on Rowe Hill in Greenwood, a short distance from where Camp Sheepskin would be built. He was best known as the Greenwood columnist for the area newspaper, reporting faithfully and interestingly on news about deer hunting every fall for years.

The third incident occurred when "one morning this week our head man went over to an old orchard, and, securing a good position, waited for big game. But he did not have to wait long. Soon down from the hill came a fine buck, and when within gun shot [shooting range], [the buck] put his

head to the ground for an apple, a bullet severed the spinal
column in his neck, when he fell so near dead as to make no
effort to regain his feet. He was a 200-pound buck and had a
perfect set of horns containing eight points."[10]

Lemuel continued reporting these kinds of hunting details
in Greenwood until he was no longer able to write. He wrote
of his neighbors' successes, failures, and hunting predicaments,
like Dannie Bryant shooting a doe while partridge hunting and
forgetting to take his knife with him;[11] a local amateur taxidermist mounting the head of a deer shot by a family member;[12]
and hunters who stopped by his farm—sometimes lost, sometimes for information, or sometimes for a bite to eat.[13] He
reported on the details of killing a deer which he had feasted
on;[14] on people who stopped by in their auto with a guide and
then went hunting, commenting that "not so much as another
hunter did they shoot in their whole tramp;[15] on the weather
and its effect on the hunting, particularly fresh snow;[16] on the
weight, number of points, sex, and other details of deer killed,
and generally how many deer were being taken in the town;
on mincemeat pie at Thanksgiving dinner;[17] on the luck of
hunters in general; and how hunters in his family would travel
miles away from home, and in the meantime, a deer would
show up in the road by the house, or a neighbor would shoot
one close by.[18]

A favorite predicament that Lemuel wrote about was the
story of the hunter who gets lost, or briefly turned around. In
one case, he reported about a man who went out one morning following a snowstorm, "and after traveling some time in
the woods, it being cloudy and the trees loaded with snow,
found himself lost; but after a while came in sight of this place

[Lemuel's], which he reached in due time, still not knowing where he was at first, although born and grew to manhood within less than half a mile of it."[19]

In the year 1914, Lemuel's column contained only one brief item on hunting, followed by this note: "Having been under the doctor's care since January, no more locals will be sent in for the present, births, marriages, and deaths excepted."[20] Two weeks later, the Locke's Mills reporter wrote: "It is to be regretted that the Greenwood correspondent is in such poor health."[21] That fall, the Locke's Mills column carried this item: "We were very sorry to hear of the death of our Greenwood correspondent, Lemuel Dunham. His items were always very interesting."[22]

Here in Maine, deer hunting stories are still found among the pages of newspapers every fall, often with photographs of hunters and the deer they have killed. Successful editors and reporters have a real, intuitive sense of what interests their readers. Lemuel grasped this, and made many trips around town to talk with people to find out what they were doing, and why. His hunting stories were timely and factual, and he didn't shy away from editorializing about the issues and trends he saw. He wrote about interesting people, humorous and tragic events in their lives, and situations that were relevant to the lives of his readers.

One story that he followed for several years touched my family. It was about a man who was most responsible for my grandfather's interest in deer hunting—his uncle Elmer Cole.

CHAPTER SEVEN

Uncle Elmer

*Lester Cole [nephew and neighbor of Elmer Cole] . . .
and his family called.*
—JULY 6, 1943, CAMP SHEEPSKIN REGISTER

I'm thinking about deer when I hear a vehicle speed up on the flat on the other side of Twitchell Pond over in Shadagee. Then it comes back to me: I'm with my grandfather in the evening in his 1930 Chevrolet coupe. It's sometime in the mid-1940s. I spent a lot of time with my grandfather then because my father was in the Philippines as part of a Navy construction battalion during World War II.

We are driving by his uncle Elmer's place in Shadagee and five deer run across the road in front of us. It was the most deer we had seen in years. It was too bad that Elmer couldn't have seen them. He loved seeing deer, and his deer hunting skills were well known in Greenwood. Elmer was home at the time, but it wouldn't have mattered. He couldn't have seen them, as he didn't have any eyes.

Of the family members my grandfather worked with on his grandfather's farm that year of 1906, he was closest to his uncle, Elmer Cole. In the lives of most hunters there is one person who encourages them, teaches them, and imbues them with a lifelong love for hunting. In my grandfather's life, this was Elmer.

Elmer loved the outdoors, and his abilities at fishing and hunting were legendary among his family. It is said that he always got his legal limit of two deer every year that he hunted.[1] Lemuel Dunham's columns for each of the two years previous to 1906 would suggest this. Elmer, he reported, shot two on the same day in 1904, hunting on snow near the end of November.[2] Again, late in the season of 1905, Lemuel wrote: "Elmer Cole was the next lucky man to take down a buck deer. He had a pair of horns containing ten points, although not a very large animal, the dressed weight being about a hundred pounds."[3] And the next year before my grandfather had experienced the excitement of shooting his deer, Elmer had already brought in two deer for the family's larder.

As a boy, my grandfather looked up to Elmer as an outdoorsman. When he was ten, his aunt Lucretia told his mother in a letter that the young hunter had "caught a coon and brought it down to Elmer to stretch."[4] He told me years later that during the year on his grandfather's farm, Elmer took him on a "real" fishing trip. No doubt the closeness of my grandfather's mother and Elmer was at the root of the relationship. Elmer was born in 1868, two years after Mary, and they were the eldest children in the Cole family. When my grandfather's mother and father lived for a short time in Dedham, Massachusetts, in 1886, Elmer, then age eighteen, wrote to them

*Photograph courtesy of the
Greenwood Historical Society*

Elmer Cole and his sister, Mary Cole, the
author's great grandmother, shown near
the end of their lives, c. 1947-48.

every week. Years later,
my grandfather often
spoke to me of his
uncle Elmer and told
hunting stories about
him. It was evident
that he respected and
cared about his uncle.
He also told me about
his uncle's terrible accident, which left him
unable to track a deer
or aim a gun ever again.

The accident hap-
pened on June 5, 1908,
two years after Elmer
had helped my grand-
father drag his deer
over Tibbetts Moun-
tain. Lemuel reported
the tragic incident in
his column:

Elmer Cole, son of Ransom Cole, a well-to-do
farmer and mill man of Greenwood Centre, was the
victim of a very serious accident Wednesday morning.

Mr. Cole was one of the road crew repairing the
highway on the Bird Hill Road, near Locke's Mills village, and had charge of blasting, in which dynamite
was used. He had set off a charge of dynamite, but it

burned out without exploding, and he then stepped forward to put a new charge in the rock and was about to attach the cap and fuse when an explosion took place and he was blown several feet away. He was picked up and taken to a neighboring house where it was soon found that the serious part of his injury was about the face and eyes, though there were several bad cuts about the body. Two doctors, Packard and Tibbetts, were summoned, and after an examination, decided to move him to the Sisters' Hospital in Lewiston.

His condition Friday was reported comfortable, with a fair chance for recovery, though doubt is expressed by the doctors as to the recovery of his eyesight. Mr. Cole is a man about 40 years of age, and has no family, making his home with his father, where he has [had] charge of the latter's mill business for several years. He is a young man well liked, and many expressions of sympathy are heard among his associates.[5]

Unfortunately, it was necessary to remove Elmer's eyes, and it had a devastating effect on him. Lemuel reported again in November that Elmer's nervous system was "badly shattered, so that it is a good deal of trouble to take care of him. It is thought doubtful if he survives the coming winter."[6] Elmer did survive the winter, but a year later, Lemuel learned that he was getting worse, requiring "someone to be with him day and night."[7]

Another year would pass before Lemuel made another report on Elmer. It was in 1910, and Lemuel had stopped by the home of my grandfather's mother; he "was pleased to find Elmer . . . on a visit there. He [Elmer] told about having his eyes removed . . . and that he had received but little benefit by submitting to the ordeal. He said the light was not so painful as to make it necessary to go blindfolded any longer, but the optic nerves were still so perfect that flashes of light were often plainly to be seen."[8]

Elmer continued to make steady progress, and in December of 1911, Lemuel wrote that Elmer "does quite an amount of work in and about the house, and appears like a different man."[9] In fact, Elmer was writing letters to his sister Maime, telling her that their brother Stant (Stanton) "got a big deer yesterday. He had a good head. Dan [Daniel, another brother] is going to have it set up."[10] Elmer's once-beautiful penmanship was still legible, despite his blindness; he wrote letters by folding the paper and using the folds to guide him.

Through the years, Elmer learned to read Braille, kept up on the news of the day, knitted mittens for nephews and nieces each winter, used a special watch to keep track of time, maintained a nice garden, raised chickens, and sold eggs for part of his living. At one time, he ran a store.[11] For many of the years following his accident, he lived alone, but in 1927 he married Minnie Black, a widow who was three years older. Minnie died in 1943, but Elmer lived another seven years, to the age of eighty-one.

A man once known for his skill as a hunter, helping his nephew drag a deer off Tibbetts Mountain, ultimately showed that he had the mettle to overcome difficulties far beyond his legendary ability to stay with the track of a deer until he got his prey, no matter the weather and terrain.

CHAPTER EIGHT

Into Manhood

Jason swamping road to cellar.
—AUGUST 29, 1944, CAMP SHEEPSKIN REGISTER

S omeone is splitting wood up on the Sheepskin Bog Road
above the camp. The sound carries easily across the
valley in the crisp morning air. This has been a familiar
sound for generations here.

My grandfather was always working with wood—cutting it,
sawing it, splitting it, selling it, burning it, or just trying to get
at it. Swamping old roads—that is, cutting out the trees that
had invaded roads in order to keep them open—was a job he
continually engaged in during his whole working life. He kept
the Old Cellar Road open that I walked in on this morning so
that he could drive his car over and take out some firewood he
was cutting. But that was not the only use of the road; in my
lifetime, a great many deer have also been dragged over it.

Perhaps it will happen again this morning.

By the time my grandfather was approaching the age of seventeen and had completed his year on Ransom Cole's farm, he had led a life that moved rapidly through boyhood into manhood. He had grown into a big, strapping young man. Plowing the rocky soils of this Maine upland was only one of the difficult tasks he had been given. Cutting, splitting, and hauling wood; haying and caring for cattle; building stone walls; and growing and harvesting crops had all been part of his long days. He had earned his $200 with room and board for the year's work. This wage was in keeping with the times—an era when the average life expectancy was forty-seven years; when most births took place in the home; when only 8 percent of the homes in the country had telephones (none had reached Shadagee at that time); when cars were an extreme rarity (there were only 8,000 in the nation, with only 144 miles of paved roads to drive on); when only 20 percent of adults in the United States could read and write; and when only 6 percent of Americans graduated from high school.[1]

His life could have been much different. While working at the Mount Abram Hotel the year before his grandfather hired him, he had taken care of the horse of a lodger. The man was a lawyer who had a firm in New York. He was impressed with my grandfather's work ethic and the way he conducted himself and carried out his tasks. At the end of his stay at the hotel, the lawyer offered to take my grandfather into his firm with the opportunity to work in the office and learn the law profession. At the time, my grandfather's mother was very ill and the family depended on him, so, as tempting as it was, he declined the offer.

The year spent on the Shadagee farm would be followed by many more on other farms and in the woods, working physically demanding jobs—straining muscles, wearing joints, and otherwise stressing his body—all of which would take its toll later in life. But despite the hard work, he never complained, and in his later years, when he was ill or wracked with pain, he worked hard not to show it. In fact, he exhibited a sense of humor that was infectious, and many friends and relatives enjoyed being in his company for that reason.

For the next two years, my grandfather worked as a teamster in the woods during winters and as a laborer on farms during summers. Then, in the winter of 1908–09, he got a job working as a cookee in a lumber camp on the side of Saddleback Mountain, a remote, wild area in western Maine. His job was to build fires in the morning, help the cook, and wash dishes. He worked eighteen-hour days, seven days a week. He was so exhausted at the end of three months that he quit. He told me that after he left he heard that the company hired three men to take his place.

Although my grandfather never mentioned it in reference to the camp he was in, the killing of deer for use as food in lumber camps was, at that time, of increasing concern to state game managers and hunters, a worry that had begun in the early 1880s. It came to a head in 1913 when a law was passed to restrict camps to six deer annually. The legislation, however, proved to be unenforceable, and it wouldn't be until 1919 that a law prohibiting the use of venison in camps would be put in place.[2]

In 1910, two events occurred that changed my grandfather's life, and their effects rippled through the lives of all of us in

succeeding generations of his family. The first occurred in
the spring of that year. "One evening," as he told it to me, "I
was stopped on a road by Mrs. Fanny Hayes, the daughter of
former United States president Rutherford B. Hayes. She and
her husband had rented a new camp on Twitchell Pond for
the summer, and she wanted to hire a cook. We talked and she
hired me." My grandfather worked for Mrs. Hayes full-time
that summer. He told me that out of that encounter and job, "a
friendship grew between our families that continued over the
lifetime of that wonderful woman."

Fanny Hayes was nearly the same age as my grandfather's
mother. She was nine years old when her father assumed the
presidency, and she lived the next four years in the White
House. When my grandfather met her, she had been married for thirteen years to her childhood friend, Harry Eaton
Smith, and they had one child, named Dalton Hayes Smith.
Sometime in the early 1900s, Fanny discovered the mountains
of western Maine, particularly the beauty of the lakes in the
region. Her earliest correspondence from Bryant Pond was
in 1909, possibly written while she was staying at a resort on
Lake Christopher run by C. Mortimer and Frances Wiske,
later called Birch Villa Inn. The summer my grandfather met
her, she and her husband had rented a new camp on Twitchell
Pond in the Shadagee area of Greenwood.

The second event occurred in December of 1910. My
grandfather, who had turned twenty that fall, married Cora
Morgan, who had grown up on Patch Mountain, in Greenwood. She was a young woman who laughed easily and was
well suited to encouraging my grandfather's sense of humor.
She liked people, and cared about the welfare of others

her whole life. When she was in her eighties, for example, she wrote to me, expressing concern that I might not have enough firewood to last through a severe April snowstorm. Her welcoming nature led to her easy acceptance into many organizations—the Eastern Star, the Grange, and other local groups—in which she was active.

She had a make-do attitude, and adjusted to the absence of many modern conveniences; for example, she dismissed the need for an indoor bathroom when she had an outhouse at the back of her barn, a convenience she maintained up until her death, at nearly ninety years of age. In her eighties, she would climb out an upstairs window in her house to shovel the snow off of her shed roof. This was during a time when she was deeply grieving the loss of my grandfather. It had been the love and devotion between these two that enabled

Family photograph

(L to R) Mrs. Fanny Hayes, daughter of President Rutherford B. Hayes and family friend, and Barbara Bennett, the author's aunt.

them to overcome the hardships they endured in their life together, and still provide the close, supportive family that I was fortunate to grow up in.

In the spring of 1911, my grandparents bought a small farm on Rowe Hill. One of their neighbors was Lemuel Dunham, who lived less than a mile away. That summer my grandmother was hired by Mrs. Hayes to cook, an activity in which she became highly accomplished. My grandfather turned his attention to the farm and took on other jobs. He cared for livestock, traded cattle and horses, raised crops, cut wood, and dabbled in selling the beef he had shipped to him from the West. Added to these jobs, he also worked in a birch mill in Bryant Pond, walking the two miles to his job in the morning and back home again in the late afternoon, where he faced an evening filled with farm chores before the prospect of getting any sleep. In a few years, his family doubled in size, with the birth of my father in 1913, and my aunt Barbara in 1917. As his responsibilities steadily increased, he pushed himself harder. The result was a nervous breakdown. He'd reached his limit, and it would be a year before he would be able to resume working.

During the decade between 1910 and 1920, when my grandparents lived on their Rowe Hill farm, the deer population in Maine continued to fluctuate from place to place in response to wood-harvesting patterns, severe winters, and, during World War I, low hunting pressure. Western Maine in these years experienced a decline in the percentage of the statewide deer kill.[3] This likely occurred in Greenwood, as well, because the human population of the town declined, from 741 in 1900 to 605 in 1920, more than 18 percent, probably resulting in fewer hunters. By the end of that decade, however, deer hunting had become a popular pastime state-wide for many people due to the social changes that led to the birth of Maine's recreational industry.[4] Hunting became recognized as a sport, and deer took on a stronger economic value.

Maine had been heading toward a sport-hunting economy for a long time. Before my grandfather was born, and since the Civil War, domestic energy had been directed toward improving the American way of life, a time we call the Industrial Revolution and the Progressive Era. Fueled by new technologies, improved methods of manufacturing, more-efficient transportation, and growing markets, the economy grew. Cities expanded, along with the attendant problems of pollution, noise, and congestion. The result: A growing affluent population started to look to the outdoors for benefits that were healthful to both mind and body.

The development of roads, modes of transportation, maps and guidebooks, and a diversity of products, from camping gear to clothing, all encouraged and helped recreationalists visit and enjoy the wild and undeveloped outdoor areas that provided refuge from the stress of civilization. Among the recreationalists were hunters of deer. They began coming to hotels and sporting camps by train in the 1800s, continuing by steamboat, horse and wagon, boat, and canoe. They were drawn by advertisements, guidebooks, and word of mouth.

They joined the National Sportsmen's Association, founded in 1875. In 1893 the Maine Sportsman's Association was founded; later, they supported a booth, organized by Cornelia "Fly Rod" Crosby, at the third annual New York Sportsmen's Show in New York, held in 1897. That same year Maine

Jason Bennett on his Rowe Hill farm, c. 1916.

began licensing guides, giving Crosby license number one. Many sportsmen were also reading *Field & Stream* magazine, founded in 1895 by John Burkhard and Henry Wack.

By the beginning of the second decade in the 1900s, a new technological advancement entered the hunting picture—the automobile. Wayne E. Reilly, writing for the *Bangor Daily News*, uncovered a headline published in a Bangor newspaper on September 23, 1911: HUNT WITH AUTOS: THE SPORT WILL BE POPULAR WITH BANGOR PEOPLE THIS FALL. The story described a "new breed of hunter equipped with tents, pneumatic mattresses, collapsible camp stoves, spirit lamps, thermos bottles, and a host of other ingenious devices. . . . One Bangor man has an automobile especially constructed for camping trips."[5]

The automobile also provided a way for hunters to carry their deer long distances to their homes, no longer having to depend on the railroads. By 1920 the use of the automobile was a news item in Locke's Mills when the correspondent for the *Oxford Democrat* reported that "several automobiles passed through here Thursday, and some of them carried deer."[6]

For my grandparents, this period of time when they were in their twenties was one of great personal and social change. As they struggled to make a hardscrabble living on a marginal farm, while raising a family, they experienced the growth of the automobile, better communications, and other advancements, all overshadowed by a brutal war. This time also led to increased pressure on deer and the need for stronger state management to protect the herd. The state's role in deer protection increased, and changes were made that affected my grandfather, coming in the form of new laws, and actions to enforce them.

CHAPTER NINE

In Defense of Deer

Don shot a spike horn buck, went home to have it tagged.
—November 20, 1960, Camp Sheepskin register

I shift my position and hear something scrape against my seat. I check to see, and it's the tag that I filled out to identify who owns the tree stand. The law now requires that tree stands be tagged in such a manner if they are on someone else's land, and permission must be given by the landowner to have a stand on his or her land. I'm also required to take my deer to a state-authorized station to have it registered within a certain time period after it is killed. These laws evolved over many years as hunting changed and the deer herd fluctuated.

When my grandfather was young, he had far fewer laws to follow, and there were also fewer wardens and enforcement methods; this would soon change, however.

Deer-protection laws and efforts to enforce them were unknown to my ancestors when Greenwood and Shadagee were first settled. Even by the time Addison Verrill and

Photograph by the author

A small doe in a field grazes peacefully out of hunting season, relying on protection by laws enforced by the Maine Warden Service.

Ransom Cole were born, there was only one law, passed in 1830, which established a hunting season from September 1 to December 31. Enforcement was almost nonexistent in those early years. With so much undeveloped land, and poor transportation limiting access to hunting areas, hunting pressure was extremely low.

By 1906, worries about a decreasing population of deer and concern over the effects of market hunting and exportation of venison, hunting with dogs, and poaching had gradually led to more laws being enacted to protect the deer herd. Laws had established that the hunting season would run from October 1 to November 30; there would be a bag limit of two deer; and no hunting was allowed on Sundays. Although my grandfather did not have to purchase a license, a new law effective that year required nonresidents to buy one. According to the commissioners' report that year, there were about sixty wardens in the Department of Fisheries and Game. "We are convinced that we have a reliable, resolute, efficient warden force, expert woodsmen of great endurance," the commissioners wrote, "but the territory to be guarded is so extensive that our whole state militia could not effectively patrol or guard it."[1]

That first decade of the 1900s also saw the beginning of mass production of automobiles. By 1920, the automobile was not only carrying hunters to their hunting destinations—it was also beginning to carry something else with it: hunting concerns. These included hunting from an automobile using headlights to jack deer, shooting deer out of windows, and carrying deer out of state to evade the licensing law.[2] These and other activities prompted the commissioners of Inland Fisheries and Game to declare in 1916 that "of all modern methods and conditions of hunting, the greatest menace [to] our game supply is automobile hunting."[3] But the agency was up to fighting fire with fire, suggesting that the Warden Service should also have automobiles to take care of poachers who used autos for night hunting.[4]

In 1919, a law was passed that prohibited hunters from having a loaded gun in their vehicle. That same year my grandfather was required to buy a hunting license to hunt deer. It cost twenty-five cents, and was good for a lifetime. The requirement was designed to keep nonresidents from hunting as Maine citizens. My grandfather was one of 84,333 Mainers to buy a license that year; the following year, 24,055 additional licenses were purchased. Around this time it was estimated that 20,000 deer were taken each year.[5]

In 1920, at the end of the first ten years of my grandparents' life together on Rowe Hill, most of the legal structure for protecting deer and managing hunting was in place; the Warden Service was becoming increasingly effective and respected; and the number of deer taken illegally was declining.[6]

By 2014, according to the website of the Department of Inland Fisheries and Wildlife, the service had grown to 124 uniformed members, working in warden districts covering the entire state. Today, the members are highly trained, certified officers who enforce laws related to inland fisheries and wildlife, snowmobiles, watercraft, and all-terrain vehicles; investigate hunting incidents and recreational vehicle accidents; promote hunter safety; and execute other responsibilities related to the mission of the agency. The department has divisions for investigation and aircraft; programs for training, whitewater enforcement, and landowner relations; teams for diving and firearms; and a K-9 unit, among other specialized activities. Members are trained in the use of specialized, state-of-the-art equipment. Among the department's wildlife responsibilities, managing the deer population is an especially important priority.

Throughout his life, my grandfather saw many changes regarding the length and duration of legal hunting seasons, bag limits, the sex of deer taken, license fees, the emergence of an archery hunting season, deer management zones, and many other laws to protect and enhance the deer herd. The state's laws and policies came to have increasing meaning to him as his own life changed, and deer hunting became more important to him—as it did to other members of his family, once he acquired his own large piece of the country in which he had grown up.

CHAPTER TEN

A Piece of Land

We combined hunting with running lines.
—NOVEMBER 30, 1946, CAMP SHEEPSKIN REGISTER

I crossed two property lines this morning when coming over
to my stand. The first, the older line, was the Old County
Road, which bounded our property at one time; the second
crossed the Old Cellar Road where it approaches the first
small stream flowing across the road into the upper end of
Sheepskin Bog. I can just see the bog down below me, almost
to the line. When my grandfather bought this property, these
two lines didn't exist. Today, both of them encompass memories of events surrounding that troubling letter we'd received
so many years ago that raised our fear about the possible loss
of our hunting privileges here.

In the early 1920s, my grandparents sold their Rowe Hill
farm and purchased a home on Main Street in Locke's Mills.
My grandfather joined the workers of the E. L. Tebbetts Spool
Company mill, just up the street from his home. Deer hunting

was as popular as ever with his fellow employees. In fact, the Locke's Mills correspondent reported early in the 1923 deer hunting season that "quite a number of the mill men are in the woods looking for big game. . . ."[1]

The move to Locke's Mills was the last move my grandparents would make. They would spend the remainder of their lives there, next to the house in which my father would live out his own life, where he and my mother would raise my brother and me. When my grandparents started this new chapter in their lives, my grandfather was the sole wage earner, and his income was meager. But they were frugal, and soon they had accumulated enough to make a purchase that would have a profound effect on their lives, and on the next generations of their family. For me, born in their house twelve years later, part of that effect would be a lifelong love for nature and deer hunting.

In 1923, my grandfather purchased 234 acres of woodland on the south side of Rowe Hill in Greenwood. Its centerpiece was, and still is, Sheepskin Bog. The bog is fifty acres in size, and extends southeastward for nearly a half-mile along the south side of the Old County Road. The name *Sheepskin* is, admittedly, a strange name for a wetland. One explanation that's been bandied about is that its shape is like that of the stretched skin of a sheep, but it's just as likely that a specific event—such as the drowning of a sheep and subsequent discovery of its remains here—led to the curious name. It will probably remain a mystery forever. However, it is a known fact that the name was given more than 150 years ago, as the bog is labeled "Sheepskin Pond" on the aforementioned 1858 map—good evidence that natural succession can turn a pond into a bog.

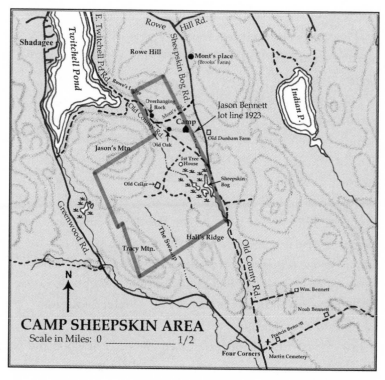

Map by the author

Jason Bennet land purchased in 1923.

Just north of the bog is a series of unnamed ridges and mountains that form one side of the bog's watershed. At their northwest end are Rowe Hill and Rowe's Ledge (called Payne Ledge on some maps), the high, south-facing, precipitous bluff overlooking Twitchell Pond and much of Shadagee. Opposite Rowe's Ledge to the south is the unofficially named Jason's Mountain. This steep-sided mountain is covered with glacial rubble and rough gray ledges, topped by white pine, hemlock, spruce, and fir. Strangely, there is a little pool of water in a low place at the top of this mountain, quietly reflecting the surrounding granite outcrops slowly exfoliating under the shade of low-branching hemlocks. From the top of this mountain, the view to the southeast fully reveals the bog in all its splendor. Along the south side of the bog is a long rise called Hall's Ridge, which stretches to the southeast from the foot of Jason's Mountain. It ends in a high bluff overlooking a swamp that runs parallel with the ridge to its south. Beyond the swamp lies Tracy Mountain, which at its southeast end also terminates in a steep, high ledge called Bald Bluff.

My grandfather's woodlot took in the whole of Sheepskin Bog and extended up onto a part of Rowe's Ledge, across to the top of Jason's Mountain, halfway up Hall's Ridge, and to the other side of the swamp at the foot of Tracy Mountain. Surprisingly, the lot—known as the Lovett Lot—had been bought by my grandfather's father in 1893, and sold by him to Ransom Cole in 1896. By the time my grandfather purchased it, the land had exchanged hands two more times, and as a result of these different ownerships, it was almost entirely clear-cut when he bought it. That's how he could afford it. In the years that followed, during the decade of the 1920s and into the '30s, the land began to recover. Its potential for timber harvesting, which my grandfather had foreseen, began to come into focus, along with another use he hadn't anticipated: a family camp.

At the time my grandfather bought the lot, he could drive his Model T Ford on the section of the discontinued Old County Road that crossed his property. If he started on the road at the lot's boundary, near the shore of Twitchell Pond, he could drive eastward across his lot to a point where the road meets the end of the Sheepskin Bog Road, a little more

Photograph by the author

The view of the Camp Sheepskin area from Rowe's Ledge looking south.

than a half-mile. At this juncture, he could go straight ahead, continuing on the Old County Road by Sheepskin Bog and eventually to Greenwood City; or, he could make a sharp left-hand turn onto the Sheepskin Bog Road and drive up the steep side of Rowe Hill by Lemuel Dunham's old farm, and, about a half-mile farther, pass the farm of his nearest neighbor, Lamont Brooks, on the top of Rowe Hill. A little ways beyond he would come to the Rowe Hill Road, where a right turn would take him by his old home and farm to Bryant Pond, or he could go straight ahead down Rowe Hill to the Greenwood Road and Shadagee. From that point, he could turn left toward Greenwood City or take a right to his home in Locke's Mills.

Thus, my grandfather's new property was surrounded by the Old County Road, Sheepskin Bog Road, Rowe Hill Road, and Greenwood Road—all unpaved roads back then. Today, the

Old County Road is discontinued and impassable, and only the Sheepskin Bog Road is still gravel; all the others are paved.

During these years, my grandfather visited the property frequently, and in the fall, he would spend some time there, hunting deer. In 1925, his bag limit for deer was reduced from two deer to one, where it has remained to the present day. By then he had already taught my father to hunt, and it was a desire have a hunting camp on the woodlot that prompted my father and his friend, Charlie Day, both in their teens, to fix up a small, deteriorating dwelling nestled under a knoll beside the Old County Road, not far from where it joined the Sheepskin Bog Road. They repaired the roof; moved in an old stove, sink, and a couple of beds; and built an outhouse. They found a spring near a small brook that flowed behind the building.

The Old Camp, as it came to be known, is not around today, but it marked the beginning of my father's lifelong love for this land. It would be a place that would reinforce his sense of strong family values, and help him to pass them on to coming generations. It would be a place where I would come to know him best—his kindliness (he would never say a bad word about anyone); his love for family gatherings and visits with friends; the pleasure he derived from cutting wood; his enjoyment of family walks in the woods that led to fishing, berry-picking, visiting old nearby cemeteries, and, of course, hunting with his family.

Across the Old County Road from the Old Camp was Sheepskin Bog, and on the Dunham farm above were apple trees. During the hunting season, deer regularly crossed the Old County Road by their camp, traveling back and forth between the bog and the apple trees. Despite this promising

Family photograph

Donald Bennett with his first deer, shot near Sheepskin Bog—1934.

hunting country and location of the camp, my father didn't shoot his first deer until 1934. By then he was twenty-one, and had been married about a year to my mother, Elsie Abbott of Bryant Pond.

My mother had graduated from the same high school as my father, Woodstock High School, after which she attended Farmington Normal School for a year, majoring in home economics. She was a happy, quiet woman, but strong-willed if she felt she needed to be. As a girl, she played banjo in the local Grange orchestra, and was active in the 4-H club. She was an excellent seamstress, and I remember that on several occasions Mrs. Hayes arrived at our house to be fitted for a dress my mother was making for her. My parents were a good match, as they both liked the outdoors and camping. My mother especially liked to study and identify wild flowers and birds, and through her long life of ninety-two years, she developed an enviable ability to identify a great many species. She and my father were also strongly connected to our community, and they actively served in several organizations.

Early in the winter of 1932, when my grandfather was forty-two, just when it seemed that his life had reached a level of comfort, with a pleasant home, secure job, happy marriage, and children nearly grown, he began to experience pain. It became so intense and debilitating that he was forced to leave his job in the mill. It was not until the next August that his problem was diagnosed as a kidney stone. Surgery was required for its removal. By winter he was able to work once again in the spool company. Unfortunately, the problem resurfaced in the summer of 1936, and following an examination at a nearby medical facility in Lewiston, he was sent for treatment at a hospital in Boston, Massachusetts. It would be the beginning of a change in his life that generations in his family would come to appreciate.

CHAPTER ELEVEN

Camp Sheepskin

Sills laid for camp.
—SEPTEMBER 8, 1936, CAMP SHEEPSKIN REGISTER

A layer of smoke drifts low over the bog between me and the ridge on the other side, beyond the Old County Road. There must be an inversion—a layer of warm air above a colder layer that is trapping the smoke from moving upward and keeping it down. The smoke is from the fires we'd built in the camp stoves well before daylight by the light of gas lamps. We'd replaced the kerosene lamps a few years ago after sixty years of use—just one of the many improvements the camp has received since it was built in 1936.

My grandfather returned from the Boston hospital weak and thin, but instead of staying home to convalesce, he decided to visit his woodlot at Sheepskin Bog, where he could cut a little firewood and regain his strength, close to the land he loved. It became his retreat for both body and soul. Every day he would take the Greenwood Road from his home in Locke's

Mills and drive his Model T Ford to the lot and a nice little
opening on the knoll above my father's hunting shack. There
he would cut wood, and when he was tired and needed a rest,
he would spread a blanket on a sunny patch of ground and
lie down. It was a quiet, peaceful location, as few people had
reason to come down the Sheepskin Bog Road or travel the
still-passable section of the Old County Road between Rowe
Hill and Greenwood City.

Over the next three weeks as he slowly recuperated, something happened. He came to realize how much he liked being
there. He began to think about having a camp right there, in
the opening, and the more he thought about it, the more he
knew he wanted it. When he discussed the idea with his family, they offered to help build it. Little did he know that he
was about to create a place that would draw generations of his
family together throughout his lifetime, and well beyond.

The camp would be less than five miles from my grandfather's home. When I was growing up, it was not unusual for
local residents to have a camp nearby. My other grandparents
on my mother's side of the family had a camp only two miles
from home on South Pond, between Locke's Mills and Bryant Pond. For many residents of these local communities, the
camps were hunting camps.

On September 8, 1936, my grandfather and father laid the
sills for a camp. Three days later lumber was delivered, and
the next day, September 12, thirty-seven relatives and friends
arrived. Many of the men were carpenters by trade. Hammers
rang, saws rasped, and beer flowed—the latter, in one case,
perhaps a little too much. My grandmother's brother Frank fell
off the roof and landed straddling a sawhorse. This put him

out of commission for a while (in one way, perhaps for life, as he never had any children). The sawing and pounding went on all day, with some respite provided by breaks for refreshment, lunch, and other necessities. At the day's end, after the din had faded and the dust had settled, a one-room camp stood in the opening. In the next few days, my grandfather and father finished the woodwork; painted the outside dark brown and the window sashes red; located, dug, and rocked up a spring; and built an outhouse, giving it the euphemistic name "the Widow Jones," one of several names for a toilet that had originated more than a century earlier. The cost for the camp: less than $100 in materials, and hours and hours of time given in the spirit of friendship and goodwill.

It was named Camp Sheepskin, after the bog one must pass by to reach it, and like birds building a nest in that wetland each spring—a piece of this, a bit of that, adjust here, move there—my family gradually shaped the camp's living space. The inside was left unfinished, with open studs and matched pine boards, which served as both outside and inside walls. A large, black, cast-iron cookstove with an oven and built-in tank for warming water was set at the front of the camp, which faced the driveway and yard. At the back of the room in each corner, two beds were placed, separated by a partition. Burlap curtains were hung on wooden rods and could be drawn to close off these quasi-bedrooms from the front of the camp, for privacy.

Between these sleeping areas and the stove were a kitchen table, chairs, a bureau, kerosene lamps, a cast-iron sink, and shelves for dishes, cooking utensils, and pails of water. A woodbox sat against the wall between the stove and door. Later, a second floor was laid over the room, creating an attic

Family photograph

Camp Sheepskin under construction—1936. The author, age one, is
sitting on his mother's lap (lower right corner).

and additional sleeping space. A ladder beside the front door went up through a trapdoor. The first floor also had a little table by the back wall, on which was placed a book containing three hundred numbered pages, bound between black

Photograph by the author

Interior of Camp Sheepskin, little changed seventy-five years after the camp was built.

covers, with the word RECORDS inscribed in gold on its maroon spine. This was the camp register, which has now grown to three volumes, where one can find a record of every visit made to the camp since the day the sills were laid.

I was one year old when the camp was built, having been born in May of 1935 in my Bennett grandparents' home where my mother and father had been staying. My parents gave me the middle name of Birchard, after Rutherford Birchard Hayes, thus extending my family's connection with Mrs. Hayes to me. From that day of the camp raising, I was present at nearly all of the hundreds of visits made by my family during the years I was growing up. Every Friday night, after my father and grandmother got home from work at the E. L. Tebbetts Spool Company mill, we would crank up my grandfather's Model T Ford (later, the 1930 Chevrolet coupe), cram ourselves into it, along with clothes, food, and everything we would need for whatever we were going to do that weekend, and rattle our way to camp. My mother told me years later how much she looked forward to those weekends, and how she hated to see them end and have to come home on Sunday evening.

A major attraction of the camp to us was its remote woodland setting. When the camp was built, much of the surrounding land was also forested, or on the way to being so. Elton Dunham was still farming nearby, but other farms in the Rowe Hill–Shadagee area were disappearing. Stone walls were beginning to enclose patches of forest rather than fields and pastures for cattle and livestock, and their usefulness would eventually rely on the quiet pursuits of those interested in history and art.

This change in the land surrounding the camp—with its old apple orchards, old fields, and patches of grassy areas, interspersed by small cuttings, cedar swamps, and a diversity of other ecosystems—created a habitat favorable to deer. The land took on a patchwork character, which, in fact, extended far beyond the borders of camp and this hilly country of western Maine. Between 1920 and 1960, almost 18,000 farms were lost in Maine, leaving the remnants of decaying buildings, collapsing fences, and rusting machinery scattered over more than 3,000 square miles of deer habitat in the state, an area equal to the size of Maine's easternmost region, Washington County.[1] These qualities of the land and its quiet peacefulness drew my family back to the camp almost every weekend for years, and still does in November for deer hunting season.

CHAPTER TWELVE

A Ghost in Hushed Tones

Elden [Hathaway] went hunting in the morning and saw two deer, but had no luck.
—NOVEMBER 10, 1938, CAMP SHEEPSKIN REGISTER

I check my watch, and while I'm doing it, I hear a sharp slap in the distance. The familiar sound carried easily through the crisp air. It's not unexpected. The slam of the camp's screen door tells me that my son-in-law is right on schedule. In a few minutes, Chuck will be walking down the Old County Road on the other side of the bog. Another half-hour, and he will have made his way around the flooded section of the road, over the beaver dam that caused it, and around the lower end of Sheepskin Bog to the camera he had set up.

Chuck had arrived yesterday filled with excitement. Impatient, he had left in the low light of afternoon in search of animal tracks, discovering a runway between a small knoll and the side of Hall's Ridge, a short distance beyond the main part of the bog. What made his blood run a little quicker was the size of one of the tracks. It was huge. He'd attached the camera to a small tree about ten feet back from the rutted trail.

93

The unit contains an infrared sensor that triggers the camera when an animal passes by, and you could tell, when he talked about it later, what he was hoping would trigger the camera— the buck that had made those tracks. This morning, according to plan, Chuck will check the camera and then stay down there until eight o'clock.

Less than a half-mile away from Chuck, I settle back against the tree. I've got some time before Chuck starts hunting. Exactly where he goes depends on the tracks and signs he sees. If he gets something moving, who knows—it might come my way. Anyway, there's plenty of time before the improbable happens, or when Chuck meets me at the Old Cellar around 8:30 a.m.

The hunting season in 1936 opened October 16, about a month after the camp was raised, and ran to November 30. Nearly 100,000 resident licenses were sold in Maine that year, a state that had a population of something over 800,000. The registered deer kill, which had been trending upward since the start of the registration system in 1919, was around 19,000, and would stay at that level for the next few years.[1]

Despite the fact that my family now had a place to hunt deer, and a fair chance of getting one, little hunting occurred at camp that fall. Most all of my family's free time was spent working on the building, the yard, and the road. The same was true for the next year, as work continued during our trips, which began in the spring. After the blackfly season, the visits became more frequent.

I was two years old that summer of 1937, and was conduct-
ing spontaneous experiments of walking and climbing under
close supervision, especially designed to keep me away from
Sheepskin Bog. (Many years later, I would venture into the
bog under certain hunting conditions with surprising success.)
In October, a path from the camp to the Old County Road
was cleared, over which we have walked hundreds of times to
Twitchell Pond, dragging many deer to camp.

Most of my family's trips to the camp in 1937 were made by
my parents and grandparents and, of course, included me, but
my aunt Barbara and her fiancé Elden Hathaway were also frequent visitors. Both of them were outgoing and pleasant, easy
people to be around. Aunt Barbara had a happy, pleasing, and
caring personality. Mrs. Hayes, who had continued her friendship with my grandparents, had known Aunt Barbara since she
was born. When Aunt Barbara reached high school age, Mrs.
Hayes employed her to help with housework at her charming
home on the shore of Lake Christopher in Bryant Pond, and
later, my aunt became her driver. The two got along very well
and became good friends. Mrs. Hayes took an interest in my
aunt's future and gave her a most unusual gift, far beyond the
financial means of my grandparents: She sent my aunt to a
nearby private college preparatory school, Gould Academy, in
nearby Bethel, where she was a dormitory student during the
four years of her secondary education.

Elden was a raconteur with a wry sense of humor that
showed up from time to time when he wrote in the camp register. The next year, in 1938, my aunt and Elden married, and
he became Uncle Putt to me. I'm not entirely certain where
the nickname "Putt" came from, but I think it was after his

Family photograph

(L to R) Elden Hathaway, Donald Bennett, and Jason Bennett at Camp Sheepskin on a hunting trip in the late 1930s or early 40s.

father, Rupert, who was also called Putt. Both of them worked on the railroad, and Rupert rode a small railway inspection car, sometimes called a putt-putt car. Years later my aunt and uncle achieved some fame as the owners of the last hand-crank telephone company in the United States, the Bryant Pond Telephone Company, which landed them on Johnny Carson's *Tonight Show* in California, all expenses paid.

I was in high school when my aunt and uncle purchased the telephone company. I worked with Uncle Putt off and on in those early years, putting up new lines, helping to install phones, and making repairs. After I had a teaching job, I worked a few weeks one summer with my uncle in the company. My aunt and uncle were always great fun to be with, something that I had known at a very early age when I went on my first deer hunting trip with them.

In 1938 plans were made by my parents and Barbara and Putt for a weeklong hunting trip at camp in November, which would include me. No one ever imagined that when the time came for the trip, we would be lucky to even get to camp, and that the woods would be changed for decades.

As fall approached, our excitement about the trip grew. On September 11, the camp register reported that we "spent the afternoon mowing and picking up the yard." It was a useless undertaking as it turned out, for at that very time a strong tropical storm system, which had originated off the coast of Africa, was moving across the Atlantic and gaining strength. It came ashore on September 21 at Long Island and then blew over Milford, Connecticut, tracking up the Connecticut River Valley. What came to be called the Great New England Hurricane of 1938 was devastating, causing 564 deaths and 1,700 injuries, destroying and damaging thousands of boats and buildings, and taking down an untold number of trees and power lines. Maine, even though it was on the fringes, suffered ravaged woodlots, severe power outages, interrupted phone service, road closures, and widespread flooding. Jason's Mountain was left covered with uprooted and downed trees, and even today hunters familiar to the area who look carefully can still see faint traces there of the storm. On October 15, my father cleaned up one spot near the camp where twenty-two trees had been blown down.

By Sunday, November 6, the road had been patched and enough trees removed to allow the five of us to come to camp for the planned hunting trip. My father and Uncle Putt were the designated hunters, with the others looking after the camp, reading, and taking walks. It was a warm week for November—a good thing, as we knew that the uninsulated camp could get extremely cold at night if the temperature was low and the fires were not kept going.

Wednesday evening we were "nearly scared to death" when a knocking occurred on the door. Being remote and at the end of the road, our camp was rarely visited at night. What's more, we had not heard any vehicle rumbling down the hill above us on the Sheepskin Bog Road. It turned out to be my grandparents, down to pay us a visit. They had left their car at the turn and walked quietly in—typical behavior for my grandfather, whose sense of humor was always with him.

On Thursday morning, my grandfather came back to hunt. Uncle Putt saw two deer but couldn't get any shots off. Even so, it was encouraging, because nothing had been seen up to that day. The next day, Armistice Day, my great-uncle Willie Morgan, one of my grandmother's five brothers, came to go hunting. The day's hunting was summed up in the register by Uncle Putt: "[W]e went hunting, but all we saw was each other." That evening, the talk turned to the one thing they *had* seen: deer tracks—and, more specifically, the tracks they'd seen of a monster buck.

I was three and a half years old that trip, old enough to pick up the change in the mood of conversation as the hunters sat around the big stove in the evening, speaking in hushed, nearly reverential tones about those unnaturally huge deer tracks. How someone had seen the awesome scrape under a hemlock at the edge of the bog, and how deep the hoofprint under it had been, pressed into bare, hard ground. It had to

Relaxing on the camp deck—1942. (L to R) The author, age seven, Cora Bennett, Jason Bennett, Bert Morey, and Elsie Bennett. The shed is completed, and the family car, a 1930 Chevrolet coupe, is at the right.

weigh 400 pounds or more to leave that kind of impression, someone said. And did you see how high up that maple sapling it had rubbed the bark off with its antlers? It had to be four feet high or more at the shoulder.

This would not be the only time I would hear about that buck. Today, nearly three-quarters of a century later, I'm still hearing about it, and no one has ever seen it. Well, that may not be true; it's a question of what stories you believe. But I and everyone I've hunted with have seen its monstrous tracks, and everyone knows, without a doubt, that it is the biggest and smartest deer that ever walked the Earth—the Ghost Buck, my grandfather called it, as I listened to the hunters talking that night in 1938. The talking went on for years, and then one year I became aware that I was doing the same kind of talking. I just knew that I was going to see this Sheepskin phantom someday; the law of averages said so. If I just hunted long enough, it would be more than just talk.

That week of hunting ended Saturday, and my grandparents came down in the afternoon and stayed for supper. The next morning, my father cooked breakfast, waking everyone up when it was ready. The forenoon was spent packing, cleaning, and visiting, and in the afternoon, someone recorded in the register: "We broke camp at two-thirty after a very fine week of camping, but the hunting was awful. Better luck next year when the two deer slayers come back for another week. —AMEN."

On September 1, 1939, the register reports: "Jason working on shed." The shed was an extension of the camp, almost as large as the first building, and all too soon it turned into another living space—the "back room," as it came to be called. There was no second floor; it was open to the rafters. It had three windows, one on each side, and one over a back door that led to the outhouse, a short distance away. Another small door was cut through from the "upstairs" of the main camp to let the air circulate. The back room contained two small corner closets with shelves, a bureau, and beds. An old parlor stove was placed out from the wall that separated the room from the main camp. Once the addition had been completed, a deck was built on the front of the main camp, which became a popular place to visit. Eventually, the blackflies forced us to close it in, and it became a screened-in porch.

The hunting trip that year could have begun on October 21, but it turned out to be much abbreviated, at least according to the expectations voiced in the register at the end of the previous year's trip. Uncle Putt and Aunt Barbara arrived on the morning of Wednesday, November 8, to stay until Friday—a little over two days. My father and grandfather did little hunting, spending their spare time working on the back room, but my grandfather was experiencing kidney problems again, which would lead to another operation the following year. The hunting result, however, remained the same: no deer.

In 1940, the camp got a resident, Herbert "Bert" L. Morey. He arrived at camp on November 2 "to cut wood for Jason Bennett." The woodlot had now recovered sufficiently from its clear-cut status in the early 1920s to be harvestable once again for pulpwood. Bert was a pleasant man with a twinkle in his eye and a face that always seemed ready to smile. He stayed at the camp and cut wood through November, and did something no one else had done since the camp had been built: On November 24, he shot a small deer.

Bert was back in mid-April to peel pulp, and worked until December 6. My family's gatherings continued as usual that year, and Bert participated in all of them: a Mothers' Day celebration, an August picnic, and a Labor Day hot dog and corn roast. Occasionally my grandfather would come down and spend a few days at camp with him and look over the cutting. Bert became a member of the family that summer, and when he completed his fall's work on December 6, the Bennett hunting "luck" had rubbed off on him: He left without having taken a deer.

The next day, our country was at war: The Japanese attacked the United States at Hawaii's Pearl Harbor.

CHAPTER THIRTEEN

The War Years

Donald home on furlough . . . came down to look at camp.
—JULY 8, 1944, CAMP SHEEPSKIN REGISTER

Below my stand, I see a big tree blown down. It's a fir, and appears from my view to be rotten-hearted. We've had several devastating windstorms in my lifetime here; I remember them because of all the trees that they blew down, preventing us from driving to camp.

One particular hard storm occurred at the end of hunting season in 1943. It downed a great many trees on the Old County Road between the Sheepskin Bog Road and the camp drive. The next summer we didn't come to camp much because my father and two uncles were in the military service, and it wasn't until August, after many trips, that my grandfather finally finished cutting up the wood in the road, allowing us to drive in. He took me with him on all those trips.

In May of 1942, Bert returned to complete his wood harvesting, and by the time he left at the end of the summer of

1942, he had spent nearly two years cutting wood on the lot. The unexpected result for my grandfather was a lifelong friendship with Bert. They shared a love for the woods, along with a similar sense of humor. One August day near the end of Bert's stay, he and my grandfather, with no small amount of enthusiasm, spent a great amount of time making a sign for a picnic my grandmother hosted at camp for her coworkers in the mill. They displayed it prominently near the outdoor fireplace, where its message would not go unnoticed: hearts broken, hearts mended, youth restored. Though they didn't intend it, this message captured what many of the family was to experience in the years ahead at the camp.

Bert's presence resulted in another new building at camp: a barn. It sat off to the side and a little behind the camp. The building housed logging equipment and Bert's horse, which he used to twitch logs out of the woods. Today, the barn houses firewood and other equipment used for maintaining the camp and the yard. In character, the building looks much the same as it did in the early 1940s. In fact, the entire camp is little changed from those years.

That November, with the camp's resident having completed his work and the camp and barn now freed up, my father, grandfather, and Uncle Putt returned for a week of hunting. The register is devoid of details except for two crucial ones: "Grand time had, but no game." By this hunting season, I was seven years old and in the third grade, and beginning to look forward to the time when I could go with them. It was a feeling that would grow with each passing year.

Three significant events happened in my life in 1943. The first occurred in June when my brother, James, was born—a major change, since for eight years I had been an only child. The previous spring my mother had given birth to another brother, Neal, but he had only lived for about two months, dying of diphtheria. Jim, however, was a big, healthy baby, and I enjoyed having him around. Despite the difference in our ages, we have remained fairly close and in touch with each other and our families throughout our lives. We have shared many interests, including deer hunting, which we still do together, and music, playing in a family Dixieland band. Jim became a college professor of music, specializing in band directing, and by a twist of fate, we both received our advanced degrees at the University of Michigan, where we studied in unrelated fields.

The second event in 1943 impressed my young mind with the potential threat of nature if it is not respected. It occurred on September 7 when I got the scare of my life. I was with my grandfather and father under the foot of Jason's Mountain, up behind the Old Cellar. We heard three loud crashes in the woods above us, so my father took a few steps in that direction and peered through the trees. What he saw was "a large bear who was in no hurry to go places."

My dad turned around and came back in a hurried, tiptoe fashion, brow furrowed. "It's a bear," he said, obvious nervousness in his voice. "There might be a cub nearby. We'd better get out of here." To me it might as well have been a charging bull moose, for I had never before been so frightened. I ran down through the woods, screaming; in retrospect, I probably frightened the bear as much as it did me. My father and grandfather soon caught up with me and calmed me down, but I never completely got over that encounter. To this day

I still experience a slight flutter of apprehension about the unknown when I'm in the woods, especially when I'm headed to my tree stand in the dark. But, strangely, it also injects a little excitement into me that I would rather have than not.

The third event, though vicarious in nature, filled me with an excitement for hunting that I had not previously known. It was a photograph displayed on the wall of our camp, along with the story of the first deer taken at the camp by a member my family. It solidified my longing for the time when I could join the family hunt. Uncle Putt chronicled it this way in the register:

> *Nov. 18, 1943.*
>
> Jason & Elden (that's me) arrived before noon on our annual hunting trip. Had dinner and went hunting a while in p.m. Came back to camp and who popped in but Willie [Bill] Morgan without his ration book. . . .

> *Nov. 19, 1943.*
>
> Got up early in the morning and Willie started to Overset [mountain] to see Roy [another of my grand-mother's brothers]. Jason & Elden hunted a while, Jason taking quite a hike. After dinner Jase and I went out again for an hour, then came back and had a nap. Woke up at 3:45 p.m. and heard three shots at 4:00 p.m. At 4:30 p.m., in came Bill on high. He shot a *big* one. At 4:45 p.m. Bill and I took a chain and started after him. At 5:00 p.m., Donald arrived and started after us. At 5:30 or 5:45, Jason started after us, got

lost and found himself. At 6:30 Roy arrived and heard excitement in woods. At 7 p.m. we all got back to camp. Had a *large* evening.

—Elden Hathaway

And Bill Morgan had this to say in the register:

Nov. 20, 1943.

Biggest hunting party and the best time I ever had; would have been wonderful if we hadn't got anything. This will be something to look back to for a long, long time. We all plan to repeat [it] in the future. . . .

—Bill Morgan, Portsmouth, New Hampshire

The next day, there was just one entry in the register: "*Nov. 21*: Moving out."

The hunting party got out just in time. A severe snowstorm hit soon after their departure, downing many trees in the camp road. It left a total of fifty-five inches of snow in nearby Berlin, New Hampshire.

Despite all of the hunting group's good intentions to get together again the following year, the hunting trip never materialized. In fact, the camp register contained no reference to hunting by the family for the next two years. The reason: My father and Uncle Putt were both overseas, serving in World War II. My uncle Robert (Bob) Farrington, who had married my mother's sister, Aunt Harriet, was also called to serve overseas. They, like my aunt Barbara and uncle Putt, lived in Bryant Pond, and were close to the family.

Photograph by Charles Martin, 2010, used by permission
Black bear photographed with a trail camera behind Camp Sheepskin near Rowe's Ledge.

Uncle Bob and Uncle Putt were both drafted into the army. My father was thirty-one at the time, and, being partly deaf in one ear, he could have been deferred. Instead, he felt a strong duty to serve along with my uncles. It didn't seem right to him to stay home, so he enlisted in the navy. Uncle Putt and Uncle Bob were stationed in Europe, and my father became a Seabee and was sent to the Philippines, where he was part of a navy construction battalion, driving a bulldozer to build airstrips.

Toward the end of the war, my father was transported to China for a planned invasion of Japan. On the boat, he met and became good friends with Donn Fendler, who, as boy, had become famous after living through a long ordeal of days lost in the Mount Katahdin wilderness of Baxter State Park in northern Maine. A popular book, *Lost on a Mountain in Maine*, was written about his miraculous survival. Nearly fifty years later, I drove my father and mother to Donn Fendler's summer home in Maine. It was the first time that the two war veterans had seen each other since that boat trip to China.

The experience of my father and uncles leaving home was terribly wrenching for them, and for all of us in our connected families. We had lived our whole lives up to that time in two small towns, among friends and relatives with strong social bonds. It was a sad and worrisome time for us, as it was for families all across the nation.

During the war years, I spent much of my spare time with my grandfather, who, in a sense, became a father figure to

Family photograph

Willie Morgan's deer—1943. (L to R) Donald Bennett, Jason Bennett, Elden Hathaway, and Willie Morgan. His deer was the first taken at Camp Sheepskin by a member of the family.

me. My grandfather's home next door was where he worked as tax collector for the town of Greenwood, and where he always seemed ready to visit with me. He often took me on trips around town when he delivered real estate tax bills, or when he had to talk with someone who was late with a tax payment. For me these were adventurous rides over the rough gravel roads, the many potholes creating a "washboard" surface. My grandfather would often strike a rock, causing the car to shimmy so much that he would have to stop. In winter, the roads could be dangerously icy. One incident on a steep section of Rowe Hill just above my grandfather's old farm left the two of us badly shaken. My grandfather, holding his breath, had to drive the car so slowly it was barely creeping over a sheet of glare ice, down a steep hill. In spring, the roads became impassably muddy, shutting down the school every year because the bus couldn't get over them.

One of the things my grandfather and I liked doing together was fishing. Pickerel fishing was a favorite, and the Greenwood Road closely followed the shores of Round Pond and South Pond—prime pickerel waters. We loved fishing for pickerel because when you jiggled a hook loaded with worms across the surface of a pond in a weedy place, you just knew that any normal pickerel would lose all caution and control over whatever sense it had. And then you would see the wake of its predatory attack, an ominous vee-shaped wave, like a torpedo, coming out of the weeds toward the ball of worms, picking up speed. You would hold your breath until it struck— a huge splash—and then it was off, your line tight, pole bent. You would watch your line go into the weeds and stop. All would be still. You would give it a few seconds, then yank and set the hook. It would fight, and even after you pulled it in and broke its neck, you could still get a nasty cut on its many sharp teeth if you weren't careful getting the hook out.

My grandfather also taught me how to trap muskrats. We both had traplines: I set mine along Alder River, not too far from my home, beyond the town dump where the stream flowed behind the church and cemetery. I baited the traps with apples. They were leghold traps set underwater and designed to drown the animals caught in them. One day I caught a raccoon. With my grandfather's help, I tanned the hide and made a coonskin cap.

My grandfather showed me how to skin the muskrats without making holes in the hides, and how to stretch them over wooden shingles for drying. At the end of the season, my grandfather got price lists from buyers, and then we got together and decided where to sell the pelts. We packed them up and shipped them off. Sometime later our checks came in the mail. Even though the return for all this effort was only a few dollars, for me, it was a partnership in big business.

My grandfather also helped me with another of my boyhood business ventures during those years of the mid-1940s: selling frogs. Every summer the town's population increased with out-of-staters who owned cottages around the ponds. Many of these visitors liked fishing for largemouth bass. The choice lure was often live frogs, especially the small leopard and pickerel frogs, called stripers because of the dark splotches on their backs and legs that from a distance look like stripes. The stripers were numerous around the grassy edges of the ponds.

I loved being around ponds, and had discovered the best places to catch these frogs. I would bike to them with a bait

pail and walk in the grass along the water's edge, scuffing and
sweeping my feet over the shoreline vegetation. The instant
a frog jumped, I would wait a moment to spot it and then
pounce on it, trapping it between my hands. I kept the frogs
in a shady, cool location in a screen-topped box containing
moss and a dish of water. Occasionally, my grandfather would
drive me to places, such as the Sanborn River in Greenwood
City, which was eight miles from home. One time I caught a
hundred frogs there. That summer I sold over a thousand frogs
for three cents apiece. Even in wartime, business goes on.

At the end of the war, my father and two uncles returned
safely, to the great relief of all of us in our family. I was ten
years old when my father returned. With my grandmother
working in the mill and my mother home looking after my
baby brother, my grandfather and I went to the railroad station every day of the week he was expected, but he was
delayed. The day he arrived, my grandfather couldn't be at the
station, so I had gone alone.

I still remember the scene when the trained pulled up to the
station and my father stepped off onto the platform, put his
arms around me, and hugged me—how happy I was to walk
beside him down Main Street toward home, keeping pace
with this tall, trim, tanned man with thick black hair carrying
his large navy satchel. What must have been going through
his mind, seeing once again the only town he'd ever lived in
after leaving with no certainty of coming back, soon to see my
mother and brother and the rest of our family. After my father
returned from the war, he never wanted to live anywhere
else—and didn't.

On October 13, 1946, my grandfather turned fifty-six, and the family had a celebration for him at the camp. The event was also accompanied by a search for deer tracks to prepare for the upcoming hunting season. Of course, the search for tracks was done with a shotgun, just in case a grouse was scared up. We followed our usual pattern—along the Old County Road to Twitchell Pond, up Mont's Road, over to the Old Cellar, and down by the Old Camp to the corner, by the Sheepskin Bog Road. We knew that along these routes there were particular places where deer seemed to prefer to cross, the same places where they would often go when "jumped," a term I learned early in my life, describing how a deer leaps away when startled. My grandfather took me on the road to the Old Cellar, and it was at the edge of the second brook that we found a huge track, which at first glance my grandfather mistook for that of a small moose. We crouched down and looked in amazement. My grandfather whispered, "I've never seen a track this size." It wasn't spoken, but we both knew what had made it: the Ghost Buck.

Life at camp seemed to be returning to normal. On November 27, the day before Thanksgiving, my grandfather, father, and Uncle Putt arrived for three days of hunting. They knew that the days toward the end of November are also the time when bucks are more likely to be seen on the trail of does, and my grandfather, who hadn't been able to get that track he'd seen out of his mind, felt that he might just see that buck this year.

The next day, they hunted hard in the morning, but without success—that is, except for one encouraging sign: a huge buck scrape behind the Old Cellar. The next day, with a freeze during the night and no snow, it was so noisy walking that they couldn't get close to a deer. My grandfather jumped two on Jason's Mountain and heard them running hard and heavy, but as much as he hoped it would be that great buck with a doe, he couldn't get his eye on the deer. He found where they had run, but there were too many leaves to see the tracks. Camp life had, indeed, returned to normal. They broke camp with no deer that year.

CHAPTER FOURTEEN

Forever Regretted

Cutting pine . . .
—SEPTEMBER 16, 1950, CAMP SHEEPSKIN REGISTER

There are no big pines anywhere near where I'm sitting. In fact, I'm sitting in a cutting that was made only a few years ago. It's probably the third time this land has been cut in my lifetime. The wood road to the Old Cellar that I'd followed this morning was once squeezed between tall white pine trees. This is what I'd always known as a boy, right up to my high school years. I loved those pines, and so did my grandfather. He might have had them cut someday, but he hadn't intended that they be on someone else's land when they were.

In the year 1947, I turned twelve, entering seventh grade in September. I was already hoping my father would take me hunting at camp that year. My father had started taking me out with him bird hunting when I was ten. He wouldn't let me carry a gun, but I was learning how to walk through the woods quietly. When I was eleven, I had accompanied my father on a day's deer hunting in Grafton, where my mother's family had a camp just on the other side of Grafton Notch. It's big, beautiful country with high, steep mountains. We hunted all morning, and when we came out to the road where we had started, I could have sworn that I was on the other side of the road. I'd gotten completely turned around. This year I was hoping that my father would take me for a day at Camp Sheepskin.

But it wasn't going to happen.

In the middle of summer, Maine was in a drought; by the middle of September, the ground was so dry that the public was being warned of the danger of fire, and told to take

Photograph by the author

A Maine fire ravaged forest, not unlike many woodlots burned during the Great Fire of 1947. Many owners, including Jason Bennett, worried about the vulnerability of their woodland property to wildfire.

preventive measures, such as no outdoor burning and no careless discarding of smoking materials. By the middle of October,
the state forest fire danger was rated as Class 4, or a "high state
of inflammability." Forest fire towers that normally closed at
that time were reopened. Then on October 17, fire broke out
and spread with a fury throughout the state, raging for a week.

By the time the fires had been controlled, nine communities
had been destroyed; sixteen people had died; 215,000 acres
of woodland and farmland had been burned, including 20,000
acres in Oxford County, in which we lived; and $30 million of
property had been lost. I listened to the reports on the radio
with my grandfather as the fire burned. To our relief, our camp
and woodlot were spared.

As a result of the fires and the fire danger, the woods in
Maine were closed from October 17 to November 12, taking a
big chunk of time out of the deer hunting season in the state.
Despite the opportunity to salvage part of the season, it didn't
occur. Another family concern had appeared at the time of the
state's ravaging fire. My grandfather experienced a return of
his kidney problem. The more immediate effect of the fire and
this health issue was the absence of any record of hunting at
Camp Sheepskin that fall.

A more serious outcome of these two concerns, which
would affect the camp and woodlot, occurred the following
year, and would threaten our opportunity to hunt there fifty
years later.

It was on August 3, 1948, nearly a year after the Great Fire,
that my grandfather did something with the camp woodlot
he would regret for the rest of his life. He was so emotionally
attached to this piece of land and would feel so badly about

what he'd done, that
all of us in the family
would be touched by
how much it hurt him.

The year had started
out as usual. I had
accompanied my father
when he made his
annual winter trip to
camp to check it out
and shovel snow off the
roofs if they needed it.
In April, as soon as the
mud season allowed,
my father, mother, and I

Photograph by the author

Jason Bennett always regretted selling
two hundred acres of his Camp Sheepskin
woodlot.

had driven to the bottom of the hill by the corner and walked
in to see how the camp had wintered. In May, I had made two
daylong visits to the camp with my grandparents. In July, I
had come with my family for a day and picked two quarts of
strawberries. Later in July, all of us had spent two weekends
at camp. But all during that time, my grandfather, who rarely
complained, had been experiencing a serious physical problem
as well as emotional turmoil.

By the middle of the summer, my grandfather was having
episodes of excruciating pain, and after a medical examination,
he learned that he needed an operation to remove one kidney.
It would have to be done in Boston, and it would be prohibi-
tively expensive. The major asset that my grandparents owned
was the camp woodlot. They could log it again, but the
amount they would get from the sale of the wood would not

pay for the medical bills. Another option was to sell it. They talked about this for days with all of us in the family, and through the discussion, it came out that ever since the Great Fire the previous year, my grandfather had worried about the loss of the woodlot to fire. The fire had impressed on him just how vulnerable a woodlot is as an economic asset. He was concerned, too, about protecting my grandmother economically if anything went wrong with the operation.

About this time, Grafton Lumber Company, which had a mill in nearby Bethel, made an offer for the property. Discussions of the dilemma ramped up as the pros and cons were mulled over by all of us. In the end, the need to be economically independent won out, and my grandfather sold nearly two hundred acres for $6,000, including a right to use the Old County Road so the company could get its wood out. It was almost all of the land across the Old County Road from the camp, which included Sheepskin Bog, Jason's Mountain, Hall's Ridge, and the swamp. He kept the forty-six acres on the camp side of the road, which went from the corner by the Sheepskin Bog Road up onto Rowe's Ledge.

From that moment until his death, twenty-two years later, he would often say to me when we were alone together at camp, "I wish I had never sold this land." I never imagined that there would be a day when I would wish the same thing, with just as much emotion.

CHAPTER FIFTEEN

Of Hunting Age

Donald, Dean, Jason, Bob Farrington, Elden Hathaway came on a hunting trip.
—NOVEMBER 20, 1949, CAMP SHEEPSKIN REGISTER

S itting in a tree stand promotes thinking, and at this moment I'm thinking about how many years I've been hunting in this spot, ever since I could carry a gun and hunt by myself. It was sixty-six years ago, in 1949, when I was first allowed to join my family's annual hunting party as an official member. It had seemed like it would never happen. Growing up takes longer when you're trying to reach an age where you're allowed to do something you've always wanted to do.

It seems like it happened just this morning.

In the summer of 1948, my grandfather had his operation, and the troublesome kidney was removed without complications. I was visiting with my grandmother when the ambulance returning him home drove into the driveway. He appeared frail and weak, but soon began to regain his strength.

That fall, the annual hunting trip finally resumed, filling its niche in the family tradition. I was still an onlooker that year when my father, Uncle Putt, Uncle Bob, and my grandfather moved in to camp on Sunday, November 21, for a week of hunting. My grandfather, though still not completely recovered from his operation, assumed the role of camp cook.

As a young boy, I was always on the periphery—watching, listening, feeling, imagining—as the camp filled with the excitement of planning, checking, packing, and preparing for each excursion into the woods beyond the tree-lined camp yard, waiting for the hunters to return, listening for the sound of gunshots beyond the thin camp walls, and seeing the deer dragged in and hung up or, more likely, hearing the stories of the signs seen or not seen and the ones that got away.

Everything was secondhand until the fall of 1949.

That autumn was significant to me for two reasons: First, I entered high school; and second, I began joining the annual family hunting party at camp. Nearly every year since that one, I have looked forward to hunting, from the time the season closed at the end of November to the beginning of the next deer season. I would begin thinking about it more and more during the spring and summer, and as the season neared, I could hardly wait for it to open.

The preparations for hunting that fall of 1949 had begun during the summer. We had several family weekend trips to camp, and among all the picnics, swims in the pond, games of horseshoes, and entertaining of visitors, we cut firewood. Most of our firewood came from dead or dying trees near the camp or along the Old County Road. We would cut the trees up and bring the wood into the camp yard, split it, and stack it for drying. Later, in the fall, we would stack the firewood in the barn, and from there, carry it as needed to a large woodbox on the porch, from which we would bring smaller amounts into the camp for each stove as the wood was burned.

Deer hunting season that year began November 1 rather than October 16. However, it wasn't until Sunday, November 20, of Thanksgiving week that our hunting party moved in. There were five of us: my father, my grandfather, my two uncles, and me. After we had unpacked, carried water from the spring, started the fires, and warmed the place up, we settled in, but not in a leisurely sense. The temperature dropped below freezing that night and every night that week, once getting as low as 4 degrees Fahrenheit. From the time we went to bed until morning, we had to get up to feed both woodstoves, just to keep everything from turning ice-cold.

The first morning, everyone was up well before daylight, and my grandfather cooked a big breakfast of bacon and eggs. We had a little snow on the ground, and it was snowing lightly, as it would do on and off all week. After breakfast, while my grandfather cleaned up, the rest of us headed in different directions, doing a quick reconnaissance for tracks. My father went up the Old County Road to Twitchell Pond; Uncle Bob surveyed the Old County Road down to the corner by the Sheepskin Bog Road; and Uncle Putt and I went over toward the Old Cellar. We regrouped afterwards. Only one set of tracks was found over by the Old Cellar, at the foot of Jason's Mountain. Back at camp, we decided to split up and hunt in different directions.

I was particularly drawn to swamps; to me, their heavy growths of cedar, spruce, and fir and beautiful mats of mosses and liverworts were dark, silent, and mysterious. I discovered that these are places where you had to keep your wits about you, for it's easy to get turned around, especially if it's cloudy and there is no sun by which to orient yourself. One small swamp is just across the Old County Road from the camp, and this is what I entered by crossing the Old County Road at the end of the path. My destination was the Old Cellar.

It would soon become an unsettling experience.

The whole swamp is probably within shouting distance of the camp, but I discovered it could still be anxiety-producing when you lose your bearings. I had dropped down into a low place, thick with cedars, when I discovered a set of deer tracks. By now the snow was falling more heavily. Before long, the

Photograph by the author

Jason Bennett resting at camp during the hunting season after his kidney operation, 1948.

tracks blended with others, and in trying to sort out the con-
fusion, I suddenly realized I had lost my sense of direction.
I knew that I couldn't be far from camp, but I had no idea of
which direction to go. It was a strange feeling, and a little scary.

I meandered along and had gone some distance when I
heard the gurgling of water running and saw a slight trickle
at my feet. I knew that there were two small brooklets that
flowed out of the swamp across the Old Cellar Road into the
bog. So I followed the brooklet, which disappeared beneath
the ground at times and resurfaced in pools and trickles. Soon
I came to a familiar place and found my way out. I was at the
foot of the hill below the Old Cellar, somewhat embarrassed
at the relief I felt when I had been so close to camp all along,
and in no danger whatsoever. Looking back on it, I'm sure that
Lemuel Dunham would have enjoyed writing about it.

I walked up the hill and turned left on a wood road we
had come to call the Tractor Road, made by Grafton Lumber Company. I soon left the road and entered the swamp
between Hall's Ridge and Tracy Mountain. It was much larger
than the small swamp I had just "survived." It was dark and
wet and thick with cedars. I knew that a brook flowed through
the center, making its way around low knolls densely covered
with firs and white pines.

I tried to keep my wits about me this time, because I knew
my grandfather had gotten lost in this swamp on a foggy day.
I hadn't gone far when I discovered the biggest scrape and
buck track I'd ever seen. The hoofprint looked like that of a
small moose. The area was dark against the snow, and when I
first saw it from a distance, I couldn't imagine what it was. But
as I approached, I knew. It was in a classic location, beneath

a huge drooping hemlock. The ground was literally torn up and the snow spattered with mud around the whole area. Even small saplings were stomped down and broken. The testosterone must have been running wild.

I just knew that it had to be the Ghost Buck. I've never been a trophy hunter, but I have to admit that the sight excited me. I made it through the swamp to Tracy Mountain and back to camp by noon that day, but I never saw another sign of that buck.

Although we hunted hard that week, we still left empty-handed on Sunday, November 27. I wrote in the register: "No deer. Had a very nice time."

This was a big understatement, because after that trip, I understood why the mill had once closed on the opening day of deer hunting season. It put me on a pattern of setting time aside to hunt at the camp for the rest of my life, with very few exceptions. Whenever I could, I would reorder my schedule of responsibilities to make it happen.

Chapter Sixteen

A Hunting Pair

[W]e heard a crash somewhere between us and the Dunham farm. My grandfather, who was standing right beside me, with a fir between us, turned to me and grinned.
—November 21, 1951, Camp Sheepskin register

The sun is right over the top of the mountain below the bog, where, nearly two centuries ago, my Bennett ancestors—Francis, Noah, and William—would have already been up for an hour or two, working in their barns before seeing the same mountain light.

A short time ago, sunlight had hit the tops of the trees across the bog from me, where the Dunham farm once stood. I remember a certain morning, about the same time of day as it is now.

My grandfather and I were standing side by side in a clump of firs along the Old County Road, below the farm, next to the remains of the camp my father had fixed up as a boy. We'd seen deer tracks there the day before, crossing the road into the bog behind us. My grandfather was wearing his dark wool pants tucked into high, laced leather boots, one gloved hand

gripping his .38-40 rifle. He was tall, over six feet, thin, and
stood up straight. He had no teeth and was usually clenching
a pipe between his gums, although there was no pipe when he
was hunting.

A stick broke in front of us. My grandfather looked over at
me with a toothless grin.

On my second annual hunting trip to camp in the year
1950, when I was a sophomore in high school at nearby
Gould Academy in Bethel, I learned a little more about my
family's hunting modus operandi. This year rain took the place
of snow the first day. Instead of spreading out and looking for
tracks, as we had done the previous year, we decided the night
before where each of us might watch the next morning; plans
would evolve according to what happened.

Uncle Putt left the record of that first day in the camp register. "J. R. Bennett & E. R. Hathaway came in on November
19 and started early this a.m. About 8:45 a.m. Jason shot at a
good deer on the southwest corner of the Lovett lot. Came in
and rained rest of day, so didn't go back."

The next day, my father and I arrived, and both of us saw
deer in the swamp, but neither could get a shot. The third
day, I climbed Jason's Mountain and jumped a deer bedded
in a blowdown oak, a remnant of the 1938 Great Hurricane.
I got a shot, but missed. A day later, my father jumped a deer
on Tracy Mountain, but it was gone before he could shoot. At
that point, my grandfather, in exasperation, decided to rectify
our bad luck in the face of so many unprofitable deer encounters. Extreme measures were needed.

He had seen deer tracks down on the "flat," as we called it—the Old County Road along the edge of the bog, leading in from its juncture with the Sheepskin Bog Road. The tracks were coming out of the bog and heading up toward the old Dunham farm's apple trees above. With a freeze predicted for that night and certain noisy conditions the next morning, my grandfather decided that the practice of getting out early should be improved upon by getting out even earlier, to be ready to catch that deer coming out of the bog.

The next morning—or it could have been the middle of the night—I heard him up rustling around. I was in the back room and could see his shadow moving through a crack in the door as he passed back and forth in the light of a kerosene lamp. Then I heard the outside door close.

Later, Uncle Putt and I were getting ready to go out to hunt, my father having returned to the mill for a day, when suddenly we heard a gunshot down by the Old Camp. I looked out the window; it was getting light. I turned toward Uncle Putt, and a slow smile spread across his face. We waited, and soon my grandfather came into camp. He wasn't happy.

"I don't understand how I could've missed," he said, his voice strained with disappointment. "I had stepped off the Old County Road into the bog, right in sight of the tracks I'd seen, and it wasn't long before I heard the deer walking toward me through the bog. The deer would take a few steps and then stop. This seemed to go on forever.

"I knew he was getting close, but my heart was thumping so hard that I had trouble hearing him. Then he stepped out right in front of me, so close that he seemed right next to me. I put up my gun, drew a bead, and fired. The deer jumped, and then within seconds I heard a couple of crashes off to my left, from where he'd come. I just couldn't have missed at that range. But I figured I should come back to camp and get some help looking."

We went back with him to look. While Uncle Putt searched for some sign of the deer, my grandfather showed me the exact place where he'd been standing when he shot, pointing to where the deer had been. There, no more than three feet directly in front of him, was a small oak tree in splinters. The bullet had hit it dead center. No deer was found, and the end of the next day, Saturday, Uncle Putt wrote in the register, "Two men went over the mountain, one over the cookstove. Same results. Broke camp in rain, [in the] p.m."

We should have had better luck that year. In 1950 there were more than 134,000 resident hunting licenses sold, nearly 15 percent of the state's population, and close to 18,000 nonresident licenses. About 77 percent of resident license holders hunted deer, and nearly all of the licensed nonresidents hunted deer, so there were about 121,000 deer hunters in the woods that fall when the four of us were hunting. That season more than 39,000 deer were taken, meaning that about one in three hunters got their deer.[1]

Good hunters try to learn from past mistakes in order to improve their hunting. The next year the focus was on my grandfather's failed and embarrassing early-morning encounter of the previous year, which, we all agreed, should have resulted in a tree in the camp dooryard with a deer hanging on it, rather than a tree down by the edge of the bog shot to splinters.

My grandfather and I arrived for the annual hunting trip on Tuesday afternoon, November 20, 1951. After unloading and opening up the camp, I made a trip over and around Tracy Mountain, and my grandfather hunted behind the Old Cellar in the lowland beyond the ridge, which he called the Hogsback.

Having no luck, we eventually met up and headed back to camp. Reaching the Old County Road by the camp driveway, we decided to check for tracks down by the Old Camp, near where the oak tree had suddenly and unselfishly thrown itself in front of my grandfather's gun to save the life of a deer. My grandfather attributed the act to the oak's indebtedness to deer for spreading the seeds of its species. As it was, the side trip to look for tracks was worth it, for we found a well-used trail coming out of the bog and crossing the road. After a brief discussion, we decided that both of us should wait there the next morning; the opportunity was too good to take the risk of having only one gun. We would have two: a 12-gauge shot-gun and a .30-30 rifle.

The next morning found us standing side by side in a clump of firs. It was still dark, but we had arrived a little later than my grandfather had the year before, on the assumption that the deer would have already crossed the road by that time and would be up at the old Dunham farm, eating apples. Our plan was to catch the deer on the way back when it was light, so all our senses were trained up the hill toward the farm.

It was just getting light enough to shoot legally when we heard a *thump* up the hill in front of us. That's when my grand-father grinned at me with a look that said he was about to get even for the unforgettable embarrassment that deer had given him last year. A few minutes later we heard a twig snap, closer by. A series of dull thuds on the frozen ground suggested that something was about to appear, and if it was, in fact, a deer, it would soon be hanging in the front yard. From the shadows among the dark firs, we detected a slight but unmistakable movement. Was this to be the moment? I had never shot a deer, and it had been years since my grandfather had taken one. My heart was hammering and pounding so wildly that I was certain it would give us away.

Another movement, and a deer stepped out. It stopped, and a silence fell over the woods as we waited. By then my gun was shaking so badly that it seemed impossible to aim it properly. Then . . . the head of the deer violently jerked up and it blew. At that moment, I pulled the trigger. *Boom!* I knew that we had the deer. Then, we heard the sound of hooves on the hard ground. We both stepped out of the firs. All was silent.

I looked at my grandfather. "Did you shoot?" I asked.

He looked at me in a funny way, and then asked, "Did *you* shoot?"

At that instant, it dawned on us: We had both fired at precisely the same moment. No wonder my gun seemed to make such a loud noise. But how could we miss at such a close range with both buckshot and a .30-30 bullet? That deer could not have gone far, but after spending the next two hours hunting for our supposed quarry, we gave up and admitted that the tree in the yard was going to be about as useless this morning as the splintered one standing on the edge of the bog.

And so it was for the remainder of the season.

Our failure down by the Old Camp did teach my grandfather and me something: We discovered that we liked waiting on a stand together. We concluded that four eyes and four ears are better than two, and there was no question but that our reaction time was the same.

So it was not surprising that the next season found us standing on the ridge behind the Old Cellar early in the morning of opening day. The ridge is sharply defined, with steep-sloped sides, beginning with a high, blunt nose that rises up from a small, swampy area behind the Old Cellar and continues in nearly a straight line up the mountain to a high knoll just under the top. The ridge was surrounded by open growth of mature hardwoods that had not been cut for years. At that time, Grafton Lumber Company had been focusing on the big pines on the lot. From the ridge, we could look through the leafless trees for a long distance in all directions. It seemed an ideal place to wait and watch, and this is what we were doing, both of us sitting on gray granite boulders—about to be tested again.

Out toward the camp, we were suddenly alerted by several gunshots, and both of us focused our attention in that direction. Soon, we saw in the distance below us two deer running through the open growth toward us. They reached the bottom of the ridge we were on and started running up directly at us. They were getting close when my grandfather opened up. His .38-40 carried at least sixteen cartridges, and his unspoken policy was that when you see a deer, you fire all of them as fast as you can.

I had my father's old .38-55, which held only four cartridges. We fired every shell we had. There hadn't been as much noise on that ridge in years, if ever. Both deer ran up the ridge, right by us, down the other side, and out of sight. We couldn't believe it; neither of them even stumbled. We were heartbroken. It was the chance we had dreamed about, and we had missed.

We started down toward the area where the deer had disappeared to see if we could find any blood or sign that we had hit one. Partway down the ridge, we met my father, who looked somewhat shaken. He told us that he had been walking on an old wood road that runs near the bottom of the ridge when he heard us shooting. He said that it sounded like a war had broken out up there. Then, he'd heard at least one deer running by, and thought he'd heard it fall.

The three of us spread out and began looking. Soon, to our great surprise and excitement, we found one deer dead and, a few minutes later, the other. A moment of jubilation ensued, but a slightly dampened one. Upon examination, we found that each deer had been hit only once. Only two shots out of a total of twenty had hit their mark. Not much to brag about as far as shooting goes, but we quickly decided that it was truly a time to celebrate, for I had shot my first deer ever, and it was my grandfather's first deer in my lifetime.

The last time we waited together, side by side, for a deer was in 1957. It happened on November 9 at 6:45 a.m. Ever since our success in 1952, my grandfather and I had continued our pattern of occasionally waiting together at some place that seemed to promise the reward of a deer. My grandfather was then sixty-seven, and despite his best efforts during the past twenty-five years, he had only been successful in that one year. His luck changed in 1957, however, during a twelve-day family hunting trip that included my mother and grandmother, who kept the camp in good living condition and provided encouragement.

Family photograph

The author and Jason Bennett shake hands after he had shot his first deer and Jason his first in twenty years while both stood side by side—1952.

We arrived on October 31, and eight days later my grandfather found an abundance of deer tracks on a trail crossing an old wood road at the end of the ridge that came down off Jason's Mountain and ended abruptly behind the Old Cellar—the same ridge where we had shot our two deer five years earlier. In fact, the old wood road, which by now had become only a trail, was the one my father had been walking up when he'd heard the first of our two deer fall. The tracks my grandfather had found came out of the small swamp of dark growth beneath the end of the ridge. That evening, we decided to repeat our strategy of waiting together, and we planned to go there the next morning.

We left the camp early and arrived at our selected spot when it was still dark. Our waiting place was beside a large glacial erratic at the edge of the road above the low, wet deer crossing. We stood together on the upper side of the boulder, which partially camouflaged us, and waited.

Sure enough, just as it became light enough to shoot, we heard a deer coming. We got ready and listened. Soon a small buck came out and stopped at the edge of the old road. Once again, we fired almost simultaneously. I've never seen a deer go down so quickly.

When we examined the deer, we determined that my grandfather's shot had killed it. What surprised us most were the antlers, the strangest-looking set we'd ever seen, all crooked and pointing in different directions, with the four points about as unbalanced as could have been possible. My grandfather was elated; my grandmother could make mincemeat again.

It was his last deer.

CHAPTER SEVENTEEN

A Family Affair

Elsie, Don, Dean, Jimmy . . . Cora, Jason . . . came to camp.
—NOVEMBER 2, 1951, CAMP SHEEPSKIN REGISTER

I look at my watch again. It won't be long before I'll be having coffee back at camp with Cheryl, Chuck, Sheila, and Rick and Karen and their two children, Abby and Nate—that is, unless our plans are interrupted by a deer encounter.

For me, deer hunting has always been a family affair. It was something we did together. It was something that we talked about throughout the year with increasing frequency as hunting season approached. Unfortunately, I wasn't able to contribute to the talking until I was old enough to hunt and acquire my own experiences, which, like a reservoir filled with water, could be drawn on when needed to sprinkle a conversation with something pertinent of interest.

On Friday, November 6, 1953, I arrived at camp from Portland, where I had started a four-year apprenticeship in cabinetmaking and architectural millwork in the Maine

Apprenticeship Program. My family was there—my mother and father, my grandparents, and my uncle Putt, although he returned home later to do some work. I would never have predicted the events that would lead to my grandfather and me tracking a deer right into the Old Cellar.

I woke up around 4:30 a.m. that day to an unbelievable racket; hailstones were coming down by the barrel full on the roof, and my grandfather was out in the kitchen, rattling every handle and cover on the stove, trying to get it going. It was freezing in the camp, so I decided to lie in bed until I was sure it was warm in the kitchen. At last I got up and looked out the window. It was still raining, and had hailed so much that the ground had turned white.

While we were having breakfast, my grandmother kept asking, "You aren't going out this morning, are you?" But out we went.

I crunched my way over toward the Old Cellar and found a place to stand. The more I waited in the freezing rain, the more I thought my grandmother was right. Finally, I just had to move, so I decided to work up toward Tracy Mountain. My feet were killing me, and felt like stilts. I kept looking down to see if I still had the gun in my hands, they were so numb. I thought that perhaps I should move over to the ridge behind the bog, so I switched in that direction toward camp.

A little farther along, I guessed that I should go over to the tree where my grandfather was standing, a little closer to camp. By now I was on the wood road to camp. It was beginning to snow. I began to think about the fire my grandmother and mother would have going. I kept walking, rationalizing that I probably didn't have enough strength in my fingers to cock my rifle even if I had to.

By the time I crossed the Old County Road, it was snowing hard. I stiff-legged my way up the drive to the camp. The stove was cranked up, and soon I was in agony with chilblains, but at least, getting warm. After having some crackers and black coffee, I headed back out on a fruitless tramp to Tracy Mountain, returning in time for lunch. Everyone was there, and we had no deer. I learned that my grandfather had fired at one, but it had disappeared into the bog.

After lunch, based on my grandfather's description of his encounter, my father began to think that maybe the deer were keeping to the bog in the storm, so he decided to take a look. About ten minutes had passed when we heard five rapid shots down by the bog. A few minutes later, my father came rushing back to camp. He told us what had happened.

He had gone beyond the camp turn to where the Old County Road ran beside the bog. As he walked along, peering intently into the bog, he had accidentally scuffed his boot on a rock. Out in the snow-covered bog, the head and antlers of a large buck appeared as the animal rose up from its bed. The deer looked right at him. My father fired right at the neck. The deer jumped, whirled, and ran. It came into sight farther down the bog, still running, and my father fired several more times before it disappeared.

We all got into our boots and put on our clothing and took off into the snow and slush. My father went back to where he had shot to look for the deer. I followed him as far as the Old Camp and then cut over to the Old Potato Field at the edge of the bog. My grandfather went off toward the Old Cellar, in the vicinity of where he had shot earlier, and could see the upper end of the bog.

This setup was based on our experience. Deer jumped in the bog would often run across the Old Potato Field or cross the Old Cellar Road at the foot of the hill, below the Old Cellar, and then go up onto Jason's Mountain.

With this in mind, I moved slowly, fully alert. I had just gotten to the edge of the Old Potato Field and was in a thick growth of firs and young pines when I came across a fresh set of deer tracks in the hailstones and snow that covered the ground. The tracks were headed toward my grandfather. I had just begun peeking and poking through the icy brush when I heard a noise. I looked up just in time to see the flash of a deer's tail. I waited, peering ahead, and in a thick maze of alders, I saw the dark shape of a deer. It began to run, bounding up into the Old Potato Field. I didn't move in case there were other deer with it.

A few minutes had passed when I heard my father shout, but I couldn't make out what he'd said. I hollered back, and after a few more times, I made out that he wanted me to come over. I took off right through the bog at a fast pace, toward where I had heard his voice. The bog heaved and bounced with every step I took, and I just hoped that I wouldn't fall through. Then I saw him just across the channel. He shouted over that he had a seven-point buck, but couldn't gut it because he had left his knife back at camp. I threw my hunting knife in its sheath over to him and told him that I was on the tracks of another one.

I hurried back toward where I'd been, and before I had gotten too far on the tracks, I was taken by surprise when I almost stepped in some blood. My father must have wounded this one when he had thought he was shooting at the buck. More blood was found as I began to track the deer. The tracks and blood went through thickets and small firs, so dense that I had difficulty getting through. The deer had crossed the Old Cellar Road in the swampy area at the bottom of the hill below the Old Cellar and circled up around behind it. I expected at any minute to come upon the deer, dead or lying down, but, instead, I met my grandfather. He had waited by the Old Cellar and had started to circle around behind it. There had been no tracks crossing the road when he had come over earlier. We decided that I'd follow the tracks of the deer and he would stay to my right, just within sight.

The tracks zigzagged toward the ridge and then turned toward the knoll behind the cellar, where I found some more blood. I saw my grandfather through the trees and waved him over. We decided the deer was nearby, so we followed the trail together toward the knoll. As we came over the top and looked down into the cellar hole below, there was the deer, standing. We took the deer there. My father's buck weighed in at 210 pounds, and the other deer, which my grandfather said I should take, because I had been on its track, was around 100 pounds. That afternoon, we broke camp with venison for the coming year for the family.

In 1955, my extended family grew: I gained in-laws when I married Luna Farrington of Bryant Pond. We had met while working for Uncle Putt and Aunt Barbara's telephone company. I was helping with the running and repairing of lines, and Luna was a switchboard operator. We established our home in Portland, where I was completing my apprenticeship.

Through the years, Thanksgiving Day and other occasions were often celebrated as a family at Camp Sheepskin (1999).

Interestingly, we both shared the same uncle, Uncle Bob, her father's brother who had married my mother's sister. I also gained two new hunting companions at camp that year: my brother, Jim, and my cousin, Michael, Uncle Putt's son.

While members of our extended family have always been involved either directly or indirectly with hunting at camp, it was Thanksgiving that often brought many of us together there, mixing hunting with the holiday celebration.

Usually my mother or grandmother would cook a turkey at home and bring it down on Thanksgiving Day, or the day before. It would be kept in the old wooden, tin-lined, slate-shelved refrigerator on the porch until reheated in the oven of our big kitchen woodstove. Those hunting would go in the morning, and toward noon, family members who weren't staying at camp would begin arriving. I remember the many times I came up the path or drive to the camp after a hard morning's tramp, weak and exhausted from exertion and hunger, to be suddenly invigorated by the sounds of laughter, happy voices, and tantalizing smells carried to me through the thin walls of the camp and the crisp cold air.

When I opened the door to the kitchen, I would be met with an overpowering blast of wood heat, joviality, and mouthwatering smells. The tiny room would be so crowded that there would barely be enough room to maneuver around the stove, sink, wood box, furniture, and toys on the floor. Over the course of the next few hours, I would tune into a dozen conversations going on simultaneously about telephone line outages, road conditions, recipes, weather forecasts, band rehearsals, deaths, births, illnesses, sports, taxes, political developments, and, of course, hunting—truly, a family affair.

CHAPTER EIGHTEEN

The Ghost Buck

[G]ot a terrific scare . . .
heard a noise, a large animal sloshing through the bog.
—OCTOBER 31, 1953, CAMP SHEEPSKIN REGISTER

I hear a thumping below me toward the bog. I'm sure it's a partridge drumming. I peer through the trees, trying to see it. I've never seen a partridge actually making the sound. It's one of those occurrences that keeps the imagination active—like the Ghost Buck.

When I first started hunting alone, I heard something on the bog that gave me a scare; it could very well have been that enigmatic creature. What I found gave me an even more impressive image of him.

At the beginning of the 1953 hunting season, on the Friday evening of October 30, my grandfather, brother, and I arrived to spend a weekend of scouting for deer tracks and other signs in anticipation of the coming deer hunt. While doing so we hoped to get a partridge or two.

What I encountered was unexpected.

Saturday morning was uneventful. My brother and I scoured Hall's Ridge, the swamp, and Tracy Mountain, while my grandfather roamed the area on the camp side of the Old County Road, jumping a small deer. We went to Locke's Mills for lunch, and all came back later, including my father, mother, and grandmother. That afternoon I decided to do a "little rabbit hunting" in the thickets along the edge of the Old Potato Field, next to the bog. That was when I got my scare—a large crash and splashing in the bog just out of my sight. I rushed out to the edge of the bog mat where I could see a long ways down the bog, and I didn't see anything.

That is, not at first.

It was when I turned back that I saw the big hole in the marsh grass at the edge of the bog. The tangle of vegetation was crushed down and mud-splattered where a deer had landed from a jump. Part of one track was visible in the muddy pocket between the grassy hummocks. It was huge. I looked in the direction of the track across the end of the bog toward the Old Cellar and saw another hole in the bog mat. I paced off the distance—about twenty feet. The next one was a longer distance away. I counted more. One was nearly thirty feet. A wave of excitement washed over me. This had to be something of a record. I told my grandfather when I got back. All he said was, "I knew that buck was still here."

The next year, 1954, my grandfather had an encounter with that buck. Deer sign was scarce around camp, so all of us were hunting around Indian Pond. When Uncle Putt, my father, and I arrived back at camp around noon, we found a note from my grandfather, who had already returned and had left for home to do some work in his job as tax collector:

> Sorry let you boys down again. See the largest
> Deer that ever walked America. I was a little late get-
> ting where I was, see him just as I stopped to look. I
> glanced to right while getting my gun to shoulder and
> see I never would see him again for so many [beech]
> leaves. Quick dropped my site on what I could see and
> pulled. Left him running at foot of Indian Pond. Let
> down again. —J. R. B. No good.

I've gone back to look at that note many times through the years as the mystery of the Ghost Buck deepened. What exactly did he see that day? I don't recall ever hearing him give more details, but I'm sure he did, for he would never let a good story lie. Today, now that I have more information and a hypothesis, there are questions I would like to ask him.

On our hunting trip in 1959, when we opened the camp door one morning to find two inches of wet snow on the ground, the first priority was to find tracks. My grandfather took the Old County Road out to the turn and down by the bog. My father decided to go up the Old County Road to Twitchell Pond, and Uncle Putt went with him as far as Mont's Road, taking the road up the hill to Mont's lower field by the Sheepskin Bog Road. I took the road over to the Old Cellar Road, and it was at the foot of the hill below the cellar, near the second brook, that I saw them—a set of enormous tracks. The front ones had to be nearly two and a half inches wide, sunk deep in the snow and mud, toes spread, pointing outward

Dean Bennett

Photograph by the author

The Ghost Buck?

and rounded, probably from scraping the ground. There were long marks where the buck's hooves dragged, all headed in a straight line, no indecision there—probably a doe somewhere ahead. My heart rate began to increase.

That buck was still here.

The tracks were easy to follow. The deer had headed down along the bog, just in from the edge through thick firs. Then I came upon a large dump of droppings, each almost an inch long, the largest I'd ever seen. They competed with moose droppings. I knew I was on the track of a deer—a huge deer. I looked intently ahead through snow-laden branches, walking slowly, watching where I put my feet to be as quiet as possible. Just beyond a large, rounded granite ledge that projected out into the bog, where I'd waited many times, the deer tracks headed out into the bog. I followed, trying to avoid wet pockets of grass and leatherleaf, and came to the edge of the brook, winding through the middle of the bog. The deer had jumped the brook. I could see that it had disappeared in one of the thick clumps of tamarack that grew in the bog.

I couldn't get across the brook, so I turned around and retraced my tracks back to camp. I reported my finding when we had all gathered to exchange information. For the rest of the day we all looked for that deer, but we never found another sign of it. What else could you expect from a ghost?

Five years passed before the next encounter occurred. It was the day my parents moved into the camp for their annual hunting vacation. My father and I spent the day hunting. I headed off to Tracy Mountain, intending to still-hunt by quietly climbing up its gradual slope on the northwest side to the top and then dropping down into the swamp to hunt through it, back to the Old Cellar. I had no more than reached the slope of the mountain and started up when I came across a rub on a beech tree. The tree was large for a rub, at least six inches in diameter. The area where the bark had been rubbed off and shredded was wide and long, as well as higher than I would have expected, and it contained deep gouges. Another sapling a few inches away also showed marks from a tine, suggesting that the deer's antlers were wide enough to reach to the other tree. The deer had thrashed smaller trees and brush nearby, breaking and bending them.

The area I was in had a number of springs, and the ground was spongy. I searched for tracks and found several. They were exceptionally large. I tried to follow, but quickly lost them in the heavy cover of dead leaves on the ground.

Then I discovered another rub on the same side of another tree. I lined up the two trees and started off looking ahead to see if I could see another rub. I had heard about rub routes but had never seen one myself. Some believe that rub trails connect feeding areas and bedding areas. I don't know about that, but the direction I seemed to be going in was toward the swamp. I searched for at least an hour but never found another rub. The signs seemed to disappear into thin air.

That noon I told my father what I'd seen, and he concluded, with a grin, that it must have been the Ghost Buck. This mystery consumed us for years. I was sure that we wouldn't know the answer in my grandfather's lifetime.

And we wouldn't . . . but we would be pointed toward a possible explanation in my lifetime.

Chapter Nineteen

The Trickster

No trouble dragging in game till p.m., when Jason shot the eye out of a doe . . . at 750 yards.
—November 24, 1950, Camp Sheepskin register

I hear a rustling sound on the slope behind me. Suddenly it stops. Seconds pass, and I hear it again. It almost sounds like footsteps. I cock my head and listen. There is definitely something there.

I slowly begin to turn my head and body around to look around the trunk of the tree. I see a movement and I tense. Then a red squirrel appears on the ground below. It scampers up the tree next to mine and sits on a limb opposite me. I shift my position slightly to see it better, and it sees me. Immediately, the squirrel begins to chatter, its tail twitching. I lift my gun to take a closer look at it through my scope. As I do so, the squirrel runs down the tree and disappears.

Then I remember.

It happened on my second hunting trip in 1950. I was in camp. My grandfather was taking a short walk up the Old County Road toward the pond to look for signs. He'd said that he would be back soon and we'd figure out where to hunt in the time left before dark. Uncle Putt was taking his afternoon nap.

Soon after he had left, I heard a gunshot, which seemed to come from near the Old Oak. About ten minutes later, my grandfather returned all excited. I met him on the porch and asked him if he had got one. All that I got from him as he grabbed a piece of rope and hurried back out was that he needed some help. I went into the back room, shook Uncle Putt to wake him, and told him that my grandfather had gotten one and needed us to help drag.

By the time we reached the Old Oak, we could see my grandfather out in the woods, slowly making his way toward us, seeming to be straining on a rope he was pulling. Uncle Putt, now fully awake, remnants of his nap brushed away by the excitement of a kill, walked hurriedly into the woods to help, and when he got close, he saw what was on the other end of the rope—a red squirrel. We all had a good laugh, and Uncle Putt, especially, because he always appreciated a good joke. Nature got back on us in the end, however, because that was the only game we got that entire hunting trip.

I learned early in my life that my grandfather was a trickster from the stories he would tell me, endlessly repeated as he sat in his well-worn captain's chair in his kitchen beneath a cloud of smoke from his pipe. I remember one, in particular.

"Did I ever tell you about the time when I was seventeen and hired out to a man by the name of Hiram Porter in South

Paris?" he would ask. I would look thoughtful, say I wasn't sure, and ask him to tell me again.

"Well," he would say after another puff of smoke drifted up, hovering over him like a speech bubble in a cartoon, "it seemed that Hiram, or Hime, as he was called, had a yen for practical jokes, and never missed an opportunity to play one. One evening Hime told me of a joke that he was planning to play on one of his hired hands that night. He wanted my help. This fellow slept in the haymow up in the barn during the summer nights, but Hime was afraid that he would set the barn on fire with his smoking. The idea was to scare the man enough so that he wouldn't sleep in the barn anymore.

"We stole some sheets from the clothesline and then found an empty grain bag and filled it with hay so that it would resemble a full bag of grain. That night around midnight, when we were sure that the fellow was asleep in the far corner of the barn, we covered ourselves in the sheets and crept to the barn. The door creaked when we opened it, and we knew that he would hear it and wake up.

"The hired hand lay in a small pile of hay, heart pounding and wide eyes straining to better see the two white figures moving toward the grain pile. He saw a light flash on, and the rays caught something white retreating toward the door, carrying what appeared to be a bag of grain. The light went out. Then he heard the muffled sound of shoes on the hay-covered floor. The light flashed on, and again a figure staggered out with another bag of grain, which was really the same bag of hay. Five, ten, and fifteen minutes passed as bag after bag of grain was seemingly removed.

"Then, the man, now shaking in the hay, heard a low voice say, 'Let's go.' He heard the sound of retreating footsteps. Then a beam of light broke the darkness. A loud whisper floated across the barn, 'Get him.'

"Almost immediately," my grandfather said, shifting in his chair, "I ran across the floor and pounced on the trembling man. I grabbed him by the throat and shouted, 'Dead men tell no lies.' I heard a peculiar gurgling noise and began to wonder if perhaps the fellow was being scared too much and the joke was going too far. I jumped up and ran through the darkness to the barn door. Outside I raced to a hiding place where I could see the front door of the house. Hime had already returned to the farmhouse, locked the front door, and taken up a position to wait.

"Just as I had settled in my hiding place, a figure streaked from the barn, shot across the yard, and leaped onto the porch. A terrific pounding was set up on the front door. This was accompanied by a loud bellowing and hollering: 'Hime! Hime! Hime!'

"Inside Hime waited a few minutes, made some noise on the stairs, and then shouted, 'Shut up your noise.'

"The poor fellow sobbed out, 'Let me in. You've been robbed of all the grain you've got, and I've almost been choked to death.' Hime unlocked the door and told him to go to bed and then stomped out to check on his grain.

"The next day the hired man talked so much that the local newspaper had a write-up about the robbery and attack, forcing Hime to estimate the amount of his loss. I guess Hime figured it was worth the trouble—the barn was never slept in again."

The author's 1952 sketch of Jason Bennett telling stories.

Having heard so many stories of my grandfather's humorous exploits, I should have been more alert to what happened on our hunting trip in 1955.

On October 31, my father, grandfather, Uncle Putt, and I moved into camp in a heavy, steady rain, and for most of the week it continued to rain, right up to the moment we moved out. The only relief we got came at the end of our first day at camp. After a morning of fruitless hunting on the camp side of the Sheepskin Bog Road, my father and I hunted during the afternoon across the road behind the Dunham farm, over toward Indian Pond. He "saw two deer but couldn't get a shot." In late afternoon, we met up and started back to camp, but I "hung up over at the edge of the cutting in just about the same place that I had shot a deer the previous year.

A half-hour went by. The rain stopped and a light mist hovered over the ground. As twilight approached and a hollow quietness settled over the cutting, I heard a sound—a scraping noise echoing over the sparsely wooded landscape in front of me. Down in the cutting to my left I saw a buck feeding. I watched the deer for a long time but couldn't get a good shot until just before dark. I fired twice, and the deer jumped and disappeared.

I scrambled down to where I'd lost sight of him, and he jumped up in front of me. I fired again, and the deer went down for good. It was just at the end of shooting time. I fired our prearranged signal just as my father was coming into the camp dooryard. He immediately recognized that it was me, got into his car, and drove up to the Dunham farm where he parked the car and came to help me drag the deer out.

It was an hour later when we got back to camp with the deer. When we arrived, something was strange. The door was locked and there were no kerosene lights on in the camp. There was no sign of my grandfather and Uncle Putt. My father got out his key and we went in.

They were not in the rooms, and all the flashlights were gone. My father was worried; he knew that my grandfather had a bad back and some heart problems, and shouldn't be out of hearing distance from any of us. We went back to the car and my father tooted the horn. He whistled and hollered. No answer was heard. Something must have happened.

We went back into the camp and did another quick search. It was dark out by then, and we needed to take the deer out to be registered. Then we saw it—a note on the table. The note said: "Out looking for two men. If they are found, fire 3 shots. E. R. H. and Jason R. B."

We hurried outside, and my father fired three shots into the air with his .30-30. From inside the camp came giggling and a voice boomed: "What the devil are you waking us up for? Can't you let a man sleep?" Then laughter.

Down the ladder from upstairs came Uncle Putt and my grandfather, who had climbed up despite his bad back. Some joke—and there were three empty shells jacked out onto the ground to prove it!

CHAPTER TWENTY

Seeing Orange

A good ending for him on the hunting trip.
—NOVEMBER 6, 1954, CAMP SHEEPSKIN REGISTER

The whole ridgeline of mountains in front of me across from the foot of the bog is now lit in bright sunlight. The big mountain that looks down on Indian Pond catches my eye, for it was there on the last day of our hunting trip in 1954 that I experienced the elation of getting my second deer in the last few minutes of the day. Uncle Putt summed it up in the register: "A good ending for him on the hunting trip."

It could have been a bad ending. What was not noted was the scare that I had gotten on that mountain in the morning, one that I had never had before, although I had always feared it might happen. It was related to the blaze orange coat and hat I have on today.

On a Saturday, November 6, 1954, the last day of our hunting trip, we started out early, before daylight. I had no light,

but in my mind I knew the route to where I wanted to go. I'd
found the place the previous day, high up on the back side of
a mountain overlooking Indian Pond.

Despite the darkness, the first part of my hike was easy:
I followed the roads. I made it to the Dunham farm, barely
making out one of the old buildings in the darkness. I took
the old road across the back field and then the tractor road
into the cutting. I had turned right on a skidder trail and just
started up the mountain when I jumped a deer. A flag bounced
and waved in the dim light, but that's all I could see. I kept
working up through the rutted, slash-edged trail. High up at
the end of the cutting, I reached a property boundary line and
the woods. It was just getting light enough to see. I left the
cutting and made my way down through open hardwoods—
beeches and oaks—where I'd seen the forest floor messed up
by deer, rooting and pawing the ground in search of nuts. I
found a place to sit with a good view and prepared for a long
wait . . . but I was not prepared for what I experienced.

I had been there for about three hours when it happened.
The gunshot came from below, fairly close. The bullet came
closer. I heard it whistle overhead, clipping through the leaves.
I dove into a depression near me and shouted. Not a sound.
It was completely quiet. I lay in the leaves for what seemed a
long time, wondering if someone had mistaken me for a deer
and taken a shot at me. I had become increasingly worried
about this as I heard the stories and read the newspaper reports
of accidental shootings. This is why I had started wearing all
red, down to my handkerchief, soon after I started hunting.

My father, grandfather, and Uncle Putt never seemed to be
too worried about being shot, but I was. My father dressed in

a green plaid jacket and hat with dark wool pants. He wanted
to be invisible in the woods. But I wasn't going to take a
chance. Even dressed in red, I felt uneasy going through thick
growth or at dusk, when the red looked black. Thankfully, this
would change in the coming years.

The hunter who sent the bullet whistling over my head
never materialized. Because I hadn't been moving and was in
relatively open growth, it's likely that the hunter was shooting
at a deer. I just happened to be beyond it in the line of fire,
or the bullet had ricocheted off something. I sat on the rock
for another hour; by then it was mid-morning. I slowly made
my way back up the hill and circled the cutting, checking for
tracks as I plotted an evening's sit. I got back to camp at noon.

Hunting accidents have been occurring since people first
started hunting. Lemuel Dunham wrote about them all the
time, and as his columns progressed through the years, his
disgust about them became more evident. On November 29,
1904, two years before my grandfather shot his first deer,
Lemuel couldn't resist editorializing: "How long will men continue to shoot each other by mistaking them for deer? One of
the most deplorable cases of that kind comes from Minnesota,
where a father shot his own son, putting two bullets through
his body, but found out this mistake when he went to the spot
and saw what he had done."[1] Lemuel may have written this
item after reading reports in other Maine newspapers about
what was happening closer to home.

The *Bangor Daily News* that fall of 1904 contained a stream
of reports about killings which were the result of mistaking
hunters for deer. On October 4, a hunter died on the way to
the hospital after being shot by another hunter who mistook

him for a deer. Before the end of the month, another hunter was killed by his brother, who'd thought he was a deer. The same kind of accident occurred on November 11. By mid-November, a total of eleven hunters had been killed and many others wounded.[2]

The situation hadn't improved two years later when my grandfather was out in the woods of Shadagee, tracking the whitetail. By the time the season was only half over, the *New York Times* reported: "Bangor, Me., Oct. 30.—Six men killed is the record thus far in the present hunting season in Maine. Last week was the worst of the year, three deaths being reported, and scarcely a day passes without the report of one or more accidents due to careless handling of guns or mistaking human beings for animals."[3]

The next season a resident of Greenwood was found dead, shot through the heart while on a hunting trip. It was perhaps the first time that a funeral had been held in the Locke's Mills Union Church for a hunting death by gunshot.[4] Lemuel posed the following question in his column at the close of the season:

> Close time on deer has once more arrived, wherefore we are glad and everybody else ought to be; but right here permit us to ask a question. In view of the fact that hundreds of men have been killed by being mistaken for deer, much valuable timber land burned over by being set on fire by hunters, and a large amount of valuable time spent in hunting that otherwise would have been put to better use, would it not have been much more wise to have put a bounty on them, like some other wild animals, instead of a close

time for protection? Please look at this question from
every point of view before answering.[5]

The problem continued to raise greater concern as the years
passed. In 1919, for example, when my grandfather was a
young man living and hunting on Rowe Hill, there were ten
fatalities and fourteen wounded. The next year there were
seven fatalities and eighteen wounded.[6] Three decades later,
in 1950, when I was a young man hunting on Rowe Hill, fifteen people had been killed and fifteen wounded in Maine
by the end of the season.[7] Two years later, in 1952, there
were seventy hunting accidents, nineteen of which were fatal,
followed by thirty-four accidents in 1953.[8] It became more
personal when I learned that my father had been missed by a
bullet passing just over his head while hunting in the woods
near our home a few years earlier, and my future father-in-law
had narrowly avoided injury when he had been shot through
the back pocket by his neighbor.

In 1959, the State began to do something about the increasing number of hunting accidents by launching a study of
Maine's hunting activities. Our camp and hunting area were
located in a test area established that year south of Route 2
and west of the Kennebec River, with an intention to study
the effect of using fluorescent gear or blaze orange to reduce
the number of hunting accidents.[9]

For the first eight years, through 1966, we hunted as usual
in the hunting clothes we normally wore. But what was different was the attention that was being given to the number
and kind of hunting accidents that occurred. Baseline data was
being gathered. When word got out about the study and the

Family photograph

Clothing in the hunting season of 1953 did not include blaze orange.
(L to R) James Bennett, Donald Bennett, the author.

idea that fluorescent orange clothing was being considered,
not everyone was happy about it. Many argued strongly that it
wasn't necessary. Others swore by the need to be camouflaged
in the woods: They didn't want people to see them, but more
importantly, they didn't want the deer to see them. They had
to be convinced that deer wouldn't become more alert when
hunters showed up in orange.

One hunter in my town wrote a letter to the editor of
a newspaper saying that anyone who was a careful hunter
would never mistake a man for a deer. The writer occasionally

160

hunted in the area near our camp, and those words came back
to bite him one November day while the study was under
way. The incident happened nearby, so close that we heard
the gunshot from camp. We thought that it was just someone
shooting at a deer; it wasn't long afterwards, however, when
I was driving up the Sheepskin Bog Road to run an errand,
that I saw an ambulance by the road. Later, we learned that
the author of the letter had shot a member of his own hunting
party by mistake. It was a nonfatal accident, but the shooter
lost his hunting license for five years.

At the conclusion of the baseline study in 1966, it was
found that 7.2 visibility-related accidents (like the one that
happened close to our camp) happened each year in our area.
For the next four years, from 1967 through 1970, we were
required to wear a fluorescent orange hat and vest; as a result,
visibility-related accidents dropped to a yearly average of 3
(one of which was fatal), a reduction of 68.4 percent. The
result was a law passed in 1973 mandating the wearing of fluorescent orange while hunting. I turned from red to orange, and
my anxiety dropped from high to low.[10]

I'm sure that my grandmother's anxiety about our hunting
was also reduced substantially by the new law. I first became
aware of her concern when I began accompanying my father
and grandfather on our annual hunting trips. She always
expressed fear for us, and was visibly worried about our safe
return.

With today's emphasis on safety by the Maine Department of Inland Fisheries and Wildlife, my grandmother would
probably feel less anxious. Maine law now requires applicants
for an adult hunting license to show proof of having held an

adult license to hunt with firearms in any year, beginning with 1976, or to successfully complete a twelve-hour hunter-safety course approved by the State. The course has a prescribed curriculum which includes proper handling of guns, especially rifles and shotguns, first aid, hunter responsibility, and other topics. Strict attendance and a final written exam are required. Additionally, game wardens promote safety and enforce laws related to safe hunting practices.

Even though my grandmother was seriously concerned about our safety, like most of the townspeople, she was not against hunting to the extent that she thought it was bad or immoral. In fact, I don't remember ever hearing anyone speak negatively about hunting when I was growing up. It was part of our lives, and certainly not considered unethical in a community where it was common to raise farm animals and slaughter them for food as part of the family diet.

Outdoor journalist and illustrator Tom Hennessey, of the *Bangor Daily News*, once wrote that in the 1950s, anti-hunting sentiment was nonexistent in his neck of the woods.[11] Lemuel Dunham's columns expressing his thoughts against hunting were published decades earlier, but they were mostly prompted by the number of deer hunting accidents. Gradually, however, as the years have gone by, society has become more urban and technologically oriented, and the direct relationship between humans and the natural world has become more obscured. New generations have abandoned some traditions, altered others, and created some of their own. Inevitably, with these changes have come changing attitudes about our responsibilities toward the rest of nature and among the voices for change, there are some that challenge the very ethics of hunting itself.

CHAPTER TWENTY-ONE

Mapping Memory

. . . documented the three recent kills on the map.
—NOVEMBER 17, 1996, CAMP SHEEPSKIN REGISTER

I started this morning by sitting in the dark, meaning that hearing quickly became my primary hunting sense— although I swear that I've been able to smell animals in the woods throughout my life. My grandfather once met a hunter near here who told him how he could always smell a deer when it was close by. Even though I'm sitting in bright sun- light now, I'm still tuned into sounds. The freeze last night left the fallen leaves crispy and noisy, and it's likely that I will hear something before I see it.

The soft, fluttering beat of a flock of chickadees suddenly takes me by surprise. One of the tiny birds flies down, lands on my knee, and begins pecking at a little speck on my pants. Then it suddenly flies up in front of my glasses and whirrs like a fan, so close that I feel a soft breeze on my face. From there it flies up onto my hat, and I can feel it walking around. It flits away as quickly as it arrived.

I look up, scan my surroundings, and rest my eye on
a mountain near Indian Pond beyond the bog where my
brother shot a deer in 1961. I know exactly where, because
we mapped the spot along with others that we got that year.
When I look at the map today, it tells me that it was one of
our most successful seasons at Camp Sheepskin.

In July of 1961, a note in the register announced: "Cheryl
Anne came down. . . . This was Cheryl Anne's first visit to
camp—age, almost 3 months." My daughter had been born
that spring, and in the fall, I had taken my first teaching job as
an industrial arts instructor at a public high school.

In the years since my own high school days, I'd always been
able to hunt Saturdays and holidays, and through the four
years of my apprenticeship, I had routinely taken a week's
vacation time in November. In college, my schedule had been
flexible enough for me to steal away for some time at camp
during the hunting season. But this fall the first serious obsta-
cle appeared that threatened this segment of time—time that
had come to have inestimable value for me, time that had to
be guarded with the same kind of vigilance given to matters of
national security, time around which a portion of my life had
been organized for as long as I could remember.

The problem was in the form of an assignment by my principal to assist in chaperoning our high school dances on Friday evenings. Camp was an hour and a half away, and it would
be difficult to do that assignment and be ready to hunt first
thing Saturday morning. Fortunately, after some maneuvering

Family photograph

The year 1961 was one of the most successful hunting years. (L to R)
the author, James Bennett, and Donald Bennett.. Each deer was recorded on a hunting map of the camp area.

and exchanging my chaperone time with other faculty, I was
able to resolve the problem.

The hunting season started with Uncle Putt shooting a
four-point buck during the first week of November. The second week my brother Jim shot a doe across the road on the
mountain near Indian Pond Tracy Mountain. The day before
Thanksgiving, my father shot a six-point buck in deep snow
toward the Greenwood Road. The day after Thanksgiving,
I shot an eight-point buck up near the pond beside the Old

County Road, which, because of the snow, I took out by boat to Shadagee across the pond.

The buck I shot that year was in the rut and on the trail of a doe. I had gone out early that morning, as soon as I could see. The snow was deep, so I was on snowshoes. I went up the Old County Road toward the pond to check out several places where we knew deer crossed the road. I snowshoed out the path and up the road by the Old Oak and Mont's Turn, and just before the Overhanging Rock, I found two sets of fresh tracks crossing the road. The deer had come down a ridge from the Rowe's Ledge area above me. I could see from the tracks that a large buck was following a doe. As I was checking the tracks, I heard something coming from where the tracks had emerged from the woods. Another large buck appeared, its head down and nose to the tracks. That's when I shot it.

The rut in Maine occurs around the middle of November. It's when we become especially alert if we see a doe. Likely as not, there will be a buck around. Many times over the years we have passed up a good doe waiting for a buck. And many times, members of our party were disappointed by this strategy. However, this has not happened to me often, because I'm not a trophy hunter. I'm more interested in venison for the table, which accounts for my universally high state of excitement when I get a deer, no matter its size. Nevertheless, I must quickly add that the buck I got that morning *did* excite me, particularly because of its size and the resulting challenge of getting it out. The isolation that the snowstorm had produced around the camp, and the need to draw on one's own resources to bring the deer back into "civilization," reminded me of the stories my grandfather used to tell about hunting in this country.

In July of 1963, my son Richard made his first visit to camp at the age of about two months. In the years to come, he and his sister Cheryl would spend a good part of their childhood vacationing at the camp—hiking, skiing, fishing, hunting, and enjoying a variety of family get-togethers on a regular basis, in all seasons. They would come to know and love it as I do, and both would become hunters of deer.

In October of that year, as the hunting season approached, I made something that we have used every year to the present, something that has come to mean more as the years have gone by. It was a map. As the hunting seasons had passed through the years and the number of deer taken had increased, the need for a visual historical record seemed necessary. It would also allow us to see if any patterns were present in our hunting successes. My decision was also influenced by opportunity. I had begun my third year of teaching industrial arts that year, and not only had a well-equipped general shop, but also a drafting room where I taught mechanical drawing. Among the pieces of equipment I had available was a blueprint machine, ideal for reproducing a large map.

To make the map, I used an opaque projector to project a topographic map onto a blank sheet of drawing paper. I then traced major features of the map onto the paper. The area to the west included the Greenwood Road, and to the east it stopped at a railroad beyond Indian Pond. The northern boundary included the Rowe Hill Road from Shadagee to Bryant Pond at the outlet of Lake Christopher, and the southern boundary included the Greenwood Road to Four Corners and the Martin Road that goes by the cemetery where my Bennett ancestors are buried. I drew topographic lines, which gave the rough shape and size of major mountains. I also included brooks, streams, and water bodies; significant buildings, roads, and trails; and major natural features.

The map was completed and a blueprint produced on October 29, 1963, just in time for that year's deer season. My family got together and went back in our collective memories to pinpoint on the map in red dots all the deer that had been taken since the camp had been built. That fall of 1963, three more red dots were added to show where deer had been taken that season.

Later, a handwritten legend was added at the bottom of the map with the names and initials of those taking deer. When someone bagged a deer, the initials of the hunter and the year of their success accompanied the red dot. Further information on the size, sex, and details of the hunt was included in the camp register. Now I can easily see where and when my father shot fourteen deer during the remainder of his life after the sills of the camp were laid.

Today, the map goes to camp with us every hunting season, and we use it often to locate some place we've been or plan to go, or something of interest we've seen. We also use it to orient friends and new hunters in our family who are unfamiliar with the area. But perhaps its best function is the stories it reminds us of. A dot on the map with a date and initials gives a reality to events that we tell over and over with humor, surprise, and suspense—stories that carry each of us back into the past, releasing our imagination, and letting us relive them, stories that we know could happen to each of us on our next trip over the mountain or into the swamp, or wherever we might go after stepping out the camp door. Such is mapping memory.

CHAPTER TWENTY-TWO

The First Tree Stand

Dean worked on the watchtower overlooking the bog.
—JUNE 11, 1960, CAMP SHEEPSKIN REGISTER

From where I sit, I can just see a tall red maple tree at the edge of the bog by the Old Potato Field. The platform at the top is long gone, rotted away and fallen to the ground. In a sense it was my first tree stand, and one from which I photographed several deer in the 1960s and '70s. But it was more than that: It pioneered the location of a number of steel and aluminum hunting stands that have since stood nearby, offering similar views.

As a boy, I wanted to be a nature photographer. I spent hours poring over magazine ads for cameras, and had looked longingly at the Japanese Topcon single-lens reflex camera. I had lain awake at night imagining the thrill of exploring the woods with that camera, capturing scenes on film for others to enjoy. But its price was well beyond my economic means. It would not be until after graduating from high school and obtaining a job that I was eventually able to afford a more-modest Yashica 35mm single-lens reflex camera, and it was at camp, high in a tree overlooking Sheepskin Bog, where I received some of my early inspiration.

I had chosen the bog as the best place from which to observe and photograph nature from a tree stand because when I was a boy, it was the most interesting. Through years of camp visits, our family had spent countless hours watching birds and animals around the bog.

I looked for a place easy to access from camp that would give a good view. The Old Cellar Road provided an easy route to the Old Potato Field, and a grown-up wood road provided a pathway down to the bog. My exploration led me to the red maple that offered a clear view for the whole length of the bog.

Here I began building a small platform thirty feet high, with access gained by steps made from oak saplings cut about eighteen to twenty-four inches long and spiked to the tree. I soon realized it would be more efficient for two people to execute my plans, with one person on the ground and another in the tree with a rope, to hoist up tools and materials, so I enlisted the help of my brother. The register tracked our project's progress that year. June 19: "Dean and Jimmy worked some on the observatory"; July 16: "Dean and Jimmy worked on the tree platform"; July 22: "Dean and Jimmy all but finished the tree platform."

It was an adventure just climbing up into the "tree house," as it came to be known. The "steps" made of oak rungs followed the twisting trunk up, three stories high. Halfway up, the tree leaned out over the climber, forcing him or her into the fearful position of tipping over backward. In summer, when leaves

were on the tree, the ground below was not visible; this gave
the climber a false sense of protection if one were unsettled by
height. But in the fall or early spring, when the tree was bare,
the distance to the ground and horror of falling were inescap-
able. The steps led up to a hole in the bottom of the platform,
through which one could squeeze and crawl out onto a three-
foot-square floor of small, straight sections of saplings and
strong tree limbs. Again, oak was used for its strength and
longevity. Heavier materials were used for supporting the platform, along with the tree limbs themselves.

Whatever difficulties we'd encountered in building or
climbing up into the tree house were quickly forgotten once
we were up there, looking out over the bog below. It was
utterly fascinating and beautiful—a place where land and
water came together, spawning an almost unimaginable natural diversity of mystery and wonder. Sheepskin Bog is one
of thousands of richly designed ecological jewels bedazzling
the Maine landscape, but this one is so amply bestowed with
these qualities that its qualifications for scenic beauty are
unquestionable. It's a wondrous wetland through which a tiny
stream meanders, fed by the two swamp-spawned brooks we
cross on the way to the Old Cellar. At the far end of the bog
from the tree house, the stream forms a wrinkle-edged pond
that balloons and collapses in size according to how much life
beavers breathe into it.

Throughout the years, a classic beaver lodge always seemed
to grace the edge of the bog's floating mat, a thick, closely
knit blanket of sedges, grasses, and sphagnum mosses, all
embroidered into the woody stems of leatherleaf, the roots of
black spruce and tamarack, and other woody plants. Beyond

Rick Bennett peers down from the tree house built in a red maple at the edg of Sheepskin Bog—early 1970s.

the open bog area, beavers, from time to time, like foresters harvesting on a regeneration schedule, create a series of small ponds to safely reach a new generation of trees and shrubs for food and construction materials. Beavers have always seemed active here. For that matter, the Sheepskin Pond of E. Swan's and Lemuel Dunham's time might have been the product of the beavers' ancestors, simply carrying on some long-held family tradition.

After I discovered how much I appreciated the view of the bog from the tree house, I soon became aware of what it's like to sit high up in a tree, not unlike what I now experience each fall in my tree stand. It's soothingly quiet, suitably remote, sublimely natural, and satisfyingly familiar. It's where I'm allowed a rare exclusivity to my thoughts and feelings—where I can think unencumbered about my life: where it has gone, where it seems to be going, and where I would like it to go. And in that year of 1960, the tree house pointed me in the direction of nature study and photography.

The camp register tells of that interest. August 5, 1961: "Dean went over to the tree house and got a movie of a hawk," and on June 10, 1962: "He [Dean] went over to the bog and sat in his tree house. At 8:15 he watched two deer down at the foot of the bog for 15 minutes. He took some movies." Many incidences were not recorded in the register, including the many hours I spent with binoculars and cameras, watching beavers, otters, and birds, in addition to deer, and one especially memorable wildlife encounter with my daughter when she was about twelve years old . It initiated her into the mysteries of the woods, and may have planted a seed of interest which would sprout years later when she took up deer hunting.

We had climbed into the tree house in the evening, and just as the last slant of light faded and darkness fell around us, we heard heavy footsteps and the crunching of brush on the ground beneath us. Then, the sound of a snort and a guttural exhalation of breath broke the silence. Cheryl looked at me, eyes wide, their whites showing in the shadows. More sounds—dull thuds on the ground below—and then nothing. We waited, our ears alert to the slightest noise. A full half-hour passed. Had the creature left, or was it still below? It seemed too quiet.

Night was upon us now, dark and scary. Neither of us looked forward to going down, especially without a flashlight. We waited some more before finally deciding to cautiously climb down. Tentatively, we stepped onto the ground, ears straining. Still no sound.

Overcoming our reluctance to leave the safety of the tree, we tiptoed away in the darkness, like cats on the prowl, all ears and eyes, following the faintly visible trail that led back to the camp, a quarter of a mile away. The sight of its windows lit by the warm glow of kerosene lamps had never looked so welcoming.

We never found out what it was we had heard that night. And even today, every time our deer hunting takes us near the tree house, we relive the experience again.

CHAPTER TWENTY-THREE

The Last Hunt

Jason came down in the afternoon. Saw only one fresh track.
—NOVEMBER 20, 1962, CAMP SHEEPSKIN REGISTER

I reach into my pocket to take out my watch. There's still some time left before we're due to meet up at the Old Cellar. I look at the watch again. It was my grandfather's. My grandmother gave it to me after he died, and I've carried it with me every hunting trip since then.

My grandfather's last hunting trip to camp took place when he was seventy-two, in 1962. It was November 20, and he stayed overnight, hunting the next morning until noon. We didn't get a deer that year.

The next year my grandparents came down on Sunday, October 6, and had lunch, leaving early to watch the World Series back at home.

By the following hunting season, in 1964, my grandfather was having kidney problems again. He'd been in the hospital that September, which resulted in an operation that placed a catheter in his one remaining kidney.

The next year he made it to camp once during our annual Labor Day outing. By 1965, he was bedridden much of the time. The catheter was often pulled out when he turned over in bed, which necessitated a hospital visit to reinsert it, sometimes causing him excruciating pain. He never made it to camp that year.

In 1967, he made his last trip to camp. He and my grandmother came down for lunch. It was November 5, when we were deer hunting.

In the summer of 1970, I lost my closest hunting companion.

The funeral was held beneath the old apple tree on my grandparents' lawn, between our homes. I was thirty-five when I stood there, viewing my grandfather's casket in the same place that my baby brother Neal's funeral was held in 1942, when I was seven—about the age of my son Rick, standing beside me. As a boy, I had often worried that I would lose my grandfather; he was so much fun, and so interesting to be around. Even though I was better prepared for his death now, there was no less sorrow.

My grandmother and I had visited him in the hospital the night before he died, and he was in so much pain that he couldn't communicate with us. We were both broken up and deeply saddened to see him that way. When I got the news of his death the next day, I was ready to accept it.

My grandfather was buried in the village cemetery on a hill behind the Union Church, overlooking the town and our homes. When I make an occasional visit to his grave, the view

Cora Bennett and Donald Bennett at Jason Bennett's grave site in Locke's Mills—1971. The home of Cora and Jason Bennett and the author's home can be seen in the distance, second and third from the left respectively.

brings back all the memories of my boyhood—of the apple tree where I spent hours watching all the people come and go as they paid their taxes in my grandfather's home. In my study, where I sit writing this, his rolltop desk holds my computer. Nearby, a framed photo shows him working at the same desk; the calendar on the wall behind him is dated 1956. On the wall in my study above this desk is the mounted head of the buck that so impressed his grandfather in 1906.

My time with him is a cherished memory. I'm fortunate to also have many good memories of my family and the times we have had together, especially those at Camp Sheepskin.

CHAPTER TWENTY-FOUR

Inroads

*Came in afternoon and found the garage had been broken into . . .some-
one stole about a pickup [truck's worth] of good dry wood.*
—OCTOBER 9, 1982, CAMP SHEEPSKIN REGISTER

I hear hammering across the bog from me. Then a vehicle
starts up and a dog begins to bark. Farther up the hill behind
the camp, a generator is running and a car door slams.

I wonder what my grandfather would say about the changes
that have occurred here since he died. He had foreseen
some—the increasing development, for example. He would
have accepted some changes with resignation, and others, he
would have fought against.

Since my grandfather's death in 1970, the camp has
changed relatively little inside and out, except for repairs
and refurbishing. The immediate lot of land it has sat on has
stayed much the same through the years.

The same can't be said about the surrounding area, where
development has made inroads in the very qualities that have

Photograph by the author

Camp Sheepskin, 1980, around a time when several acts of vandalism occurred.

continued to draw us to the camp through the years—its remoteness, solitude, and stillness, its feeling of wildness and of stepping back in time.

By the time my grandfather died, there were three or four camps on the Sheepskin Bog Road above the camp. Two were owned by the descendants of Lemuel Dunham and his son Elton. Today, there are five year-round homes. One is on the old Dunham farm, above our camp turn off the Sheepskin Bog Road, on the ridge overlooking Sheepskin Bog.

These new dwellings brought road improvements and utility lines. The Sheepskin Bog Road was upgraded down to our turn, where it was enlarged so that the town snowplow and a school bus could turn around. The sounds of human activity increased within earshot of the camp—doors slamming, dogs barking, motors running, and traffic traveling up and down the road. It wasn't long before we saw joggers on the Old County Road by the camp, along with all-terrain vehicles (ATVs), sightseers, and cats and dogs.

These changes were not totally unexpected; they have been happening innocently and normally for years throughout rural Maine and elsewhere. They are still occurring as the human population enlarges, maps become more prevalent and sophisticated, utility and all-terrain vehicles become more affordable and specialized, and people become more affluent and technologically advanced. For us, they were not as disruptive as the changes affecting the Old County Road, which was closer to our camp.

By the 1960s, the Old County Road along the east side of Twitchell Pond had been upgraded, lots sold, and camps constructed along the shore of the pond. The road was still impassable beneath Rowe's Ledge, but that changed in the late 1960s and early '70s. A religious group, the Northeastern Gospel Crusade, built a retreat camp beside the Old County Road near the beach on Twitchell Pond, rebuilding the road beneath Rowe's Ledge to access it. By the mid-'70s, the retreat facilities had been abandoned, but the road past our camp was now open to through traffic.

It was also open to vandalism.

Between 1980 and 1988, we had ten break-ins. Doors were jimmied, locks broken, and windows smashed. One time when my parents went to camp for wood, they saw the doors open to the camp and barn. In the back room a window had been removed and someone had stolen the stove, five lamps, and

Donald Bennett stacking firewood at Camp Sheepskin—1981. It was at a time when break-ins and stolen firewood became a problem.

numerous smaller items. The sheriff came to investigate. My parents started their own investigation by visiting used furniture and appliance stores in the area. They found their stove. My father had scratched his navy service number on the stove in an obscure place. The burglar was eventually tracked down and arrested. Another time, someone broke into the barn and stole enough wood to fill a pickup truck.

The break-ins caused much time, energy, and money to be expended in cleaning up, repairing, and replacing the damaged and stolen items. Psychologically, the invasions resulted in many unsettled feelings and worry, especially in my mother and father. My father put up no trespassing signs on the road to try to prevent the unwanted access. My parents made many trips to camp just to check on it. As they drove into the camp dooryard each time, they experienced great apprehension about the condition in which they would find the camp.

The camp road—that is, the section of the Old County Road that we drove over to get to the camp from the Sheepskin Bog Road—also became a problem. People began rutting it up by driving over it too early in the spring, before it had dried out sufficiently to hold up a vehicle. ATVs, especially, left deep ditches in the surface of the road that my father worked to fill every year, and on several occasions, he found ruts in the wetland along the side of the road, as well as out in the bog. The no trespassing signs had no effect.

The camp invasions and road problems continued throughout the 1990s, along with other issues. A note in the register

Photograph by the author

Rick and Cheryl Bennett looking at ruts in the Old County Road near Camp Sheepskin.

spoke of the increasing sounds penetrating the walls of the camp: "[H]eavy construction equipment. Civilization moves closer." One day I received a shock when I was hunting Jason's Mountain and looked up to see a no trespassing sign in front of me deep in the woods on a boundary line in a place where I had routinely passed on my way up the mountain. (I learned later that this was a result of a boundary dispute.) Cheryl was surprised one morning when a dog walked by her stand. Another time when we were hunting, I was waiting one early morning off the Old County Road and heard something running by. It turned out to be a jogger on the road. We "encountered *more* garbage (many beer bottles, empty cigarette packs, etc.) and the remnants of a campfire at the turn."

We talked about putting up a gate all through the 1980s and '90s, but my father didn't want to go that far; in fact, none of us did. Then came that day in May 1999, when we discovered what we had feared the most: For about a half-mile on our property, the Old County Road—from our turn at the Sheepskin Bog Road nearly to Twitchell Pond—had been developed. And not by the logging company, which held the only other deeded right-of-way, apart from ours.

CHAPTER TWENTY-FIVE

A Matter Unsettled

Road has been regraveled from the turn up toward the lake . . . We will have to investigate.
—MAY 23, 1999, CAMP SHEEPSKIN REGISTER

I hear a vehicle come down the hill and slow down at the camp turn. A few moments later a car door slams. The gate creaks. I feel a slice of resentment, but it's gone as quickly as it came, long replaced by resignation. The car door slams again. Soon I hear the vehicle going up by the camp on the Old County Road. I make a mental note to alert Cheryl and Chuck that there may be hunters staying in one of the houses up near the pond.

The incident began on a bright, sunny day in May of 1999, when my eighty-six-year-old mother, my wife Sheila, and I drove to our family camp for an outing, and to check out how the camp had wintered. Rick followed us in his vehicle.

We came down the back side of Rowe Hill on the Sheepskin Bog Road and turned the corner onto the Old County

Road. Expecting to see the rutted, vegetative-cramped, primitive-looking road it had been becoming, we were astonished to see a new "highway"—a broad strip of freshly dumped gravel, packed, smoothed, and pushed out into the muck and swale of the bog on one side and to rough, rock-strewn woods on the other. I stopped the truck abruptly. We were stunned. What had happened?

We began to drive slowly on. Where nature had once pushed itself to the edge of the lane, new metal culverts sparkled; fresh-cut, sap-seeping stumps on our land glistened orange; and huge boulders lay blasted to bits and shoved aside along the edge of the road, an invitation to traffic that I had not imagined. This was our camp road—a narrow, memory-filled pathway where our vehicles crawled over deepening ruts, beneath drooping branches, and between encroaching trees; where every spring for nearly sixty-five years we had checked to see if it was passable after winter had taken its toll; where my grandfather and father would then clean out ditches, unclog decaying wood drainage boxes, and remove wind-downed trees and branches, always keeping nature close, their eyes peeled for evidence of spring—the pink flower of lady's slipper; the white, red-splashed petals of painted trillium; or the yellow blossoms of bead lily. The expected condition of the camp road was symbolic of what we cherished about our "camp in the woods"—a place of respite found in nature. Had my father lived three years longer, he would have known and sounded the alarm, perhaps preventing the shock waves that spread through our family.

We drove on the new road past our camp drive, by the Old Oak, by Mont's Road, by the Overhanging Rock, to where our line crosses the road near the ledges, and there the road turned abruptly left toward Jason's Mountain, dipping down through the swampy stands of hemlocks and firs that lie at the foot of the mountain, and turning left up along the steep, southern shore of Twitchell Pond. Here, one could catch glimpses of the pond, Shadagee on the other side, and Rowe's Ledge across a cove. Behind us logging was occurring on Jason's Mountain, and a side road led to a landing near the foot of the mountain. We took all of this in, and slowly drove back to camp to try to fathom it all and decide what to do.

It turned out to be the work of a logger-developer, who had purchased property on Twitchell Pond for its timber, and for the sale of waterfront camp lots. This immediately raised our concern, because we believed that this would mean the new owners of the lots would likely want to use the road by our camp for access to their properties.

That summer and fall, meetings and phone calls took place and letters were exchanged with the logger-developer, and, eventually, between our lawyers as we tried to resolve the issue of access to the new camp lots. We hoped the issue could be resolved by having the new lots accessed from the Twitchell Pond end of the Old County Road—but this didn't work out.

The key question, of course, was, did the logger-developer have a legal right-of-way on the Old County Road through our property? In the late 1930s and early '40s, my grandfather had thought that his ownership of the discontinued Old County Road across his property had been settled following an argument with the owner of the property, whose heirs had sold it to the logger-developer. Since that time, my grandfather had given one right-of-way to the logging company that had bought most of his land on the south side of the Old County Road.

This question of right-of-way ownership became the focus of attorneys and hired legal experts. A variety of settlement proposals were presented by both parties, but not accepted by one or the other. By the November 1999 hunting season, there was still no resolution in sight, and traffic by our camp was continuing to increase, with sightseers and workers coming to the new camps. Our attorney notified the logger-developer and the lot owners, now a total of six, that we would be gating the road. This we did.

The result: Court action was brought for a preliminary injunction to remove the barriers. During the court proceedings, my mother took the stand to convey to the court what the camp meant to her and our family, and to put the change in the road and the traffic it invited into the context of the emotional ties to the land and the camp we had developed during her sixty-four years of visits there. Despite her testimony, and Rick's and our lawyer's arguments, the judge granted the preliminary injunction and ordered the removal of any impediment to the plaintiffs having access to their property, pending final judgment or further action of the court. It was still not over, as the question of whether the plaintiffs had a legal right-of-way remained unresolved.

Through the following winter, spring, and most of the summer, efforts to settle between the parties were not successful. As a result, our attorney filed a court motion for a judge to decide on the facts of access without a trial, called a summary judgment. The court hearing was held in early September 2000, and found that the logger-developer and owners of the land sold to them would need to prove that a public prescriptive easement existed for them to access their property over

A section of the Old County Road near Camp Sheepskin—(L) 1971—
Cheryl Bennett taking a favorite family walk, enjoying the road's
little-traveled, historic, primitive-appearing character and (R) 1999—
the road following her family's stunning discovery of its widening and
development.

the Old County Road. Such an easement could exist if the road
had a history of public use meeting certain legal conditions.

It seemed likely that we were headed to trial court.

At this point the issue took a new turn. The logger-developer was able to purchase about forty-five acres across the
Old County Road from our camp—land originally part of my
grandfather's lot, which he had sold in the late 1940s. By the
time deer hunting season arrived, we had been informed that
we could purchase this land in exchange for a right-of-way
across our property on the Old County Road to the developed
property on Twitchell Pond.

Near the end of the month, we received a letter with a
settlement offer that we took seriously, but it also raised an

alarming concern. We believed that if a settlement could not be reached a road might be built running parallel to the Old County Road in front of our camp; and that the land could perhaps come to be owned by someone in the future who might not be willing to give us hunting privileges.

In December, we agreed to purchase the land that my grandfather had once owned in exchange for giving a right-of-way on the Old County Road to the other parties. By the end of February 2001, the issue had been settled, the gate had once again been closed, with keys for all parties legally using it, and the road blocked at the other end near Twitchell Pond. The break-ins stopped, quietness returned, except for the occasional vehicle going by, and we could now hunt on our own land to the top of Jason's Mountain, just as my grandfather had once done on his land.

It was over for us.

One day in March I drove down to camp. The road was plowed from Mont's Place at the top of Rowe Hill down to the turn, and someone had plowed up to the new camps on Twitchell Pond. I unlocked the gate, drove through, locked it again, and drove up to the camp drive, where I shoveled enough to get the truck off to the side of the road so someone could get by. I skied up to the camp, unlocked the door, and built a fire in the stove. I had planned on shoveling off the porch roof, but there wasn't enough snow to worry about. After the camp had warmed up a bit, I brewed some coffee and had a biscuit. It was quiet except for the crackling fire in the stove, and with the exception of the gaslights, the camp had the same look, smell, and feel that it had had when I was a boy.

It was easy to drift back in time. I could hear my grandfather's voice, a slightly strained sound with a soft rasp, telling me how he shouldn't have sold his land here, his face downcast, a sadness I can still clearly remember. I thought about the letters I have kept—letters from the late 1930s and early '40s that show how my grandfather resisted the pressure to allow a right-of-way through this property.

How would he have felt about the trade-off we had made to deed a right-of-way to the current owners of that land, in exchange for some of that land he had bemoaned the loss of? We had doubled his forty-five acres to ninety, which now took in the top of the mountain he loved. Behind his love for this land, he had a practical mind. He was a horse trader while still a boy, and knew that you often didn't get everything you wanted in a deal. There was a give-and-take on both sides. I think he would have agreed we did the right thing under the circumstances.

After coffee, I closed up the stove, put on my skis, and headed toward the Old Cellar. It was March corn snow, and I sailed over the old road. On the knoll by the Old Potato Field, I looked up to the top of Jason's Mountain on my right. The old pines along our line seemed to stand tall and proud, knowing they were too important a part of the scene to ever be cut by their new owners.

I came down the hill to the first brook flowing into the bog and saw something white sticking up out of the snow at the edge of the brook. At first I thought it was a limb that had been cut, its bark gnawed off by beavers, but it was too white and smooth, its point too rounded. I approached it and stooped over to get a closer look. It looked like the tine of an antler. I scraped out the snow around it, grasped it with one hand, and pulled. It moved slightly, so I kept digging, deeper and deeper.

Finally, out from the snow came the largest set of deer antlers I'd ever seen. There were six stout and long points, and two were divided. Some tines were slightly webbed between them. The diameter of the beam was unusually large where it attached to the skull. But what struck me most was the condition: One tine was broken off and another cracked; there were chips and nicks in many places. This wasn't the work of mice and other rodents. These were scars from battle. Now the antlers lay discarded in the snow, their work done. A new set would grow this coming spring to do battle again.

In a way I wish we could shed our battle scars so easily, but I expect they will be with us for a long time. I looked up at the mountain. I knew what my grandfather would have said: "That buck is still around and doing battle. Maybe some things don't change too much."

That summer of 2001, we initiated a forest management plan to do a thinning cut of the land to help pay our legal expenses, and to pay for the land we had purchased. The years following the road issue continued to produce changes in our surroundings. The remainder of the large lot that my grandfather once owned, out of which we gained the forty-five acres, was sold to a large investment company that logged the land around the Old Cellar and beyond, and used their right-of-way on the Old County Road. But the company kept us informed and cut the timber responsibly, in a sustainable manner. Today, we have permission to put up tree stands and continue to hunt on the property.

CHAPTER TWENTY-SIX

Unbroken Tradition

*Chuck Martin and Cheryl Bennett arrived from Illinois. We were met by
Donald & Elsie, Dean, and Rick. . . . Aah! It's great to be in Maine and
participating with family.*
—NOVEMBER 6, 1988, CAMP SHEEPSKIN REGISTER

Two ravens fly over with their "oinking" talk. They are
headed toward Cheryl, in her stand under the mountain. She's shot several bucks from that stand since
she and Chuck started hunting here in the late 1980s. Cheryl,
Chuck, and I just celebrated twenty-seven years of hunting
together here.

From the time of my grandfather's death, I have hunted
with members of my family nearly every fall to the present. Although much has remained the same, there have been
changes.

During the 1970s, the camp was the scene of archery hunting every October, followed by gun hunting in November.
I had started archery hunting in 1969 with my good friend

Family photograph

(L to R) The author, James Bennett, and Rick Bennett, on an archery hunting trip at Camp Sheepskin—1970s.

and former college classmate, Wayne Stearns. He had grown up in nearby East Stoneham, and was an educational media specialist with a local school district. His brother Don and my brother Jim eventually joined us for the archery season. Throughout that time, my mother and father continued taking a week's vacation at camp in November.

194

The camp saw other changes during that decade. Rick and I rebuilt the tree house at the edge of Sheepskin Bog in 1971. During the summer of 1975, the camp became a place of recuperation for me, as it had for my grandfather nearly forty years earlier. That spring I was diagnosed with a severe case of mononucleosis. The cure was plenty of rest.

By then Luna and I had divorced, and I had married Sheila O'Toole Seymour, who also had two children, Regan and Tanya, from her previous marriage. She had instantly been taken with the remote, quiet, simple beauty of the camp and its surroundings, and we decided that the camp offered the perfect place for me to convalesce. Rick stayed with us, and Sheila's children were there for periods of time. I spent weeks lying down, so weak that I could barely hold a toothbrush. I lost most of the feeling in my hands and feet. Late in July, my strength began to return, and by the first of September, I was able to return to work.

The first half of the decade of the 1980s at Camp Sheepskin saw little hunting. My grandmother died in 1982 at the age of eighty-nine, in good health right up to her last week. She had always been a coalescing figure for our camp's family get-togethers. Uncle Putt did not hunt at all in the '80s; my father did not hunt deer in 1983 and 1985, and only once in 1984, although he and my mother made many visits to camp throughout those years, as they had always done. My brother Jim was teaching music in Vermont by then, and he no longer hunted in Maine. My son Rick was in college. Without someone to hunt with at camp, my interest waned; I hunted very little, and then only around my home in Mount Vernon, where I shot two bucks during those years.

One of those bucks weighed 219 pounds field-dressed, and was the second-largest deer shot that year in Mount Vernon. In the town, many deer are weighed and tagged at the Country Store in the middle of the village. Each deer tagged is recorded on a poster placed in one of the store's front windows, including the size of the deer, sex, and name of the hunter. I was new to town that year, one of those "from away." I wondered then if getting that deer—in a town where success in shooting a deer, especially one that size, is noticed—helped me to advance a notch toward being seen as maybe not from too far away. Maybe I was fanaticizing, but I'd grown up in a town about the size and character of Mount Vernon, and had a pretty good idea about how people thought and communicated.

Despite my success in hunting around my home in Mount Vernon, it wasn't the same for me. It became increasingly apparent to me that my love for hunting was closely tied to the social experience of being with my family at camp, hunting together in the pursuit of deer, spending good times with each other in a place cut off from the rest of the world, where life was simple and relied on few modern conveniences.

In 1986, I hunted one day with my father, Rick, and my good friend and neighbor, Jim Hall, a cardiologist turned writer who, with a keen sense of humor, was producing some witty and entertaining books about fishing. Deer hunting was new to him. We had arrived on a Friday afternoon with Sheila and my mother. During the hunt, the only wildlife seen was a mouse and a shrew, which I claimed, and even that was disputed. My father hunted only one other time that fall.

Later that fall, just when the future of deer hunting at Camp Sheepskin was looking bleak, I got a phone call at home from

Cheryl—a call that would not only lead to a revival of deer hunting for all of us at camp, but would also inject us with some new blood, new enthusiasm, and, for me, a new way of hunting.

Cheryl was in northern Wisconsin working as a civil engineer for the Federal Highway Administration. She had been assigned there for six months in an internship program for new employees of the agency. She had called to tell me she was in love with a young man named Charles

Photograph by the author

Cheryl Bennett and Charles Martin begin hunting at Camp Sheepskin, 1987.

Martin, who would come to be known to us as Chuck. Chuck was a member of the Lac Courte Oreilles Band of the Lake Superior Chippewa Indians, and had spent part of his youth on the tribe's reservation. He also had spent time as a boy with his grandparents, when his grandfather worked as a guide for a sporting camp. I would soon learn that Chuck was keenly woods-wise, and a skilled and enthusiastic deer hunter.

Chuck took Cheryl deer hunting that fall in Wisconsin, and she shot her first deer, a small buck. After that, deer hunting became a passion for her. It came as a great surprise to me. As a girl she had never shown much, if any, interest in going hunting with me, although she liked the outdoors, and had

197

accompanied me on many hiking, canoeing, and cross-country skiing trips in the mountains and North Woods of Maine. It had been Rick who had always wanted to go hunting. But now I had a daughter who wanted me to go hunting with her, so she joined the list of other women hunters I have known.

After Christmas that year, Cheryl and Chuck came to Maine, and on New Year's Day, 1987, the two skied down the back side of Rowe Hill so that Cheryl could show him the camp. She took him into the back room where we had put up the antlers of every buck taken since the camp had been built. She showed him the old photos on the wall of the many family get-togethers with my grandparents, the big old iron cookstove, the kerosene lamps, the woodshed, the neat-looking outhouse, and the location of the spring. With his rural upbringing, Chuck felt right at home. But what was different for him, what he was most struck by, was the terrain—the steep hills and high ledges that surrounded the camp. It was unlike the low-rolling, flatter land he was accustomed to. He fell in love with it, and would come to know it intimately in the coming years.

That year of 1987 we took a hunting trip at Camp Sheepskin, and from then on our love for deer hunting and the camp has drawn us back there every November. For the next few years, hunting at Camp Sheepskin became like the old days for me. Every fall while my father was alive, Cheryl and Chuck would arrive from Wisconsin for a week or two of hunting, met by my parents, beaming with excitement. The camp would be warm, clean, and orderly, everything in readiness. Sheila and I would arrive, along with Rick and his wife, Karen, and we would have a family luncheon to launch the season, to which we always invited Uncle Putt and Aunt Barbara.

It wasn't long before Uncle Putt got caught up in the new enthusiasm for deer hunting that enveloped the camp, and he started hunting again in the fall of 1989. The increased hunting activity and fun we were having pulled him in. He was seventy-two that season when he joined my father, then seventy-six, for a morning's hunt on opening day. For the next three years, through 1992, he visited almost every day we were there, arriving in his van dressed in his hunting garb, whereupon he would visit for a few hours, have a cup of coffee, and then take a short walk with his gun. He always entertained us with his stories, views on current events, and humor, sometimes playing a musical tune with his deer call that hung around his neck. When he died in 1993, he left a big void in our hunting party. My aunt Barbara continued to join us for a family luncheon at camp at the beginning of our annual hunting trips until her death, ten years later.

In 1990 I shot the first deer that I had ever shot from a stand. Chuck had hunted from stands for many years in Wisconsin, and he and Cheryl had begun bringing several stands with them. They had both climbing stands and stationary ladder stands. Through the following years, we purchased more stands, and today we sometimes have as many as eight stands set up. Some are kept up permanently, and others are moved around as logging operations, new roads, and increasing settlement on Rowe Hill change the patterns of deer movement.

The 1996 hunting season was one of our best. We opened it with a special celebration at our annual camp luncheon, noting our tenth anniversary of hunting together and Rick's election to the Maine Senate. It was also my granddaughter Abigail's first visit to camp during the hunting season. She is

Rick and Karen's daughter. Three and a half days later, Cheryl, Chuck, and I each had taken a buck. Our luck was infectious.

Rick appeared one day with a thirst to hunt, as did Ron Martin, Rick and Cheryl's stepfather. They knew him as Mr. Martin when he was their music teacher in high school, and after he married Luna, they began calling him "Mr. M." Now many of us just call him "M." My father also experienced a resurgence of his desire to hunt with the sight of so many deer hanging up, and he made several trips with his gun up the Old County Road by the Old Oak.

My parents were regular visitors in 1996. At eighty-four, my father still appeared vigorous. Four years earlier, in the winter, he had snowshoed to camp down the hill from Mont's Place, putting up the ladders and shoveling off the roofs. So I was unprepared for his death the next month. It was at the end of December that he and my mother caught the flu, and he died from complications. Among his last words to me as he lay delirious in his hospital bed: "I'll meet you over on the ridge behind the Old Cellar."

In 2004, I got a small doe, which allowed me to spend time bringing our map up-to-date. The locations, dates, and names of all our deer kills were checked, and all those that had faded over time were retraced in ink. That fall we also examined our other two records—the camp register, and the antlers mounted on the walls of the back room. As of October 13, we had made 103 entries in the third volume of the register. In our survey of the back room, we counted 27 sets of antlers.

Our annual hunting trips continued in their well-established family tradition. In 2006, we missed my mother at our annual venison luncheon; she had passed away that spring at the age of ninety-two. She had been in attendance for nearly every luncheon, and was the last of her generation to be at camp. The hunting season the year she died was for Cheryl, Chuck, and me the twentieth anniversary of our hunting together.

In 2008, I got to hunt with my brother after his absence for many years. He and his wife Julia both retired that year and moved from Vermont to nearby West Paris. Living only twenty minutes from camp, he was with us often, and we spent many delightful hours together, reminiscing.

The year 2010 was one of great excitement for us, and one of much activity around the camp. We learned in late 2009 that Cheryl had been selected as the new assistant division administrator for the Maine office of the Federal Highway Administration. By then she had worked twenty-four years for the agency.

On January 19, 2010, she and Chuck came to Maine to look for a home in the Augusta area. They ended up living temporarily in Rick's cottage on Lake Christopher in Bryant Pond, about ten minutes from camp. Chuck, who had been employed in the housing market for many years, was affected by the deep recession and was unemployed. For several years, we had been aware that the camp needed major repairs and other work, so that spring, Chuck, with time and skills, began working on a broad array of projects.

At camp, one of Chuck's first projects was making a loop trail on our property that encompassed both sides of the Old County Road. After the trail was completed, he and "M" worked together throughout the summer to repair and refurbish the camp and our big cookstove, with a little bit of help from Cheryl, Sheila, and me. They gave the stove a thorough cleaning, installed new parts, and put in a stainless-steel, insulated stovepipe. After leveling the camp and porch, they sided and stained both. Today, we have propane gaslights, which were installed under the supervision of "M" to replace our kerosene lamps. We still have the original outhouse and a spring, which supplies us with water for washing, but we now bring drinking water in jugs from home, or from a roadside spring in Bryant Pond.

That year, our friends Regina Webster and John Richardson came to spend a few days hunting with us, a rare event, and one we had all looked forward to. We first met them and became good friends when they leased and ran Nugent's Chamberlain Lake Camps, a historic sporting camp owned by the State of Maine in the Allagash Wilderness Waterway. Later, they sold their lease and bought their own camps, McNally's Ross Stream Camps, near the Allagash's Long Lake, fifty miles farther north. In the first decade of this century, the number of deer declined precipitously in the area around their camps, to a point where they were getting no deer hunters as guests. So we invited them to spend a few days with us each season.

At the end of the season, with the camp spruced up and looking almost as new as it did when it was first built, still relatively unchanged in appearance, we decided that a celebration was in order. The next fall, on Sunday, September 4, 2011, nearly eighty people who had been associated with the camp over the past seventy-five years came to celebrate what it had meant in their lives. For me its meaning was best summed up by one of our older guests, who said to me as we sat talking before lunch: "This is the way we used to get together as families. I wish it was done more." With this remark, my mind went back to my boyhood and all the photos we have of my grandparents'

(L to R) The author, Rick Bennett, Abigail Bennett, Nathaniel Bennett, Ronald Martin on a hunting trip at Camp Sheepskin—2012.

friends and family visiting together, sitting on the deck that eventually became the camp's porch. Among them was a photo of a young girl, my grandmother's niece, who is the wife of the elderly man who spoke to me that afternoon.

Later, after the celebration, and at the beginning of deer hunting season, our family gathered for the twenty-fifth year that Cheryl, Chuck, and I have hunted together, accompanied most of those years by Rick, and many years, by "M." The next morning, opening day, "six hunters went into the woods," and among them was my grandson Nate, Rick and Karen's son, who represented the latest generation of hunters in our family, a generation with a dwindling number of deer hunters.

Visits to camp had started early for my two grandchildren. Nate's first visit to camp was on July 12, 1998, when he was less than four months old. His sister, Abby, first visited on November 10, 1996, at the age of ten months and three weeks. My nephew, Jason, came on October 9, 1977, at the age of two, with his father, Jim, when he was bow-hunting. Later in his life, Jason would hunt with us occasionally. Chuck's two boys, Tyler and Casey, my two step-grandsons, made their first visits to camp when they were old enough to hunt. They joined our annual hunting trip on November 8, 1998, at the ages of twelve and thirteen.

On an early morning in the 2012 hunting season, I took Abby with me to Cheryl's stand under Jason's Mountain. She never accompanied us with a gun; instead, she just wanted to be with us to see whatever came by. She sat on a rock at the bottom of the stand, perfectly quiet and attentive. The woods were in a deep freeze, and after an hour, I whispered down to her, "What do you think about going back to camp for a cup of coffee?" Within three minutes, we were on our way back.

Later that afternoon, I took Nate up toward the ledges on Chuck's trail behind the camp. I could tell that he had the makings of a good hunter. He handled the gun carefully, walked stealthily, took in his surroundings, and frequently stopped to listen and look. What role the camp and these surroundings will play in their lives and in the lives of Chuck's boys and other members of my family, I'm unable to imagine. I can only hope that this camp, or a place like it, will be a part of their lives, enriching theirs as it has mine with family, friends, and perhaps, a little mystery.

CHAPTER TWENTY-SEVEN

A Ghost in the Shadows

[It] crashed around . . . blowing constantly . . . sounded extremely heavy and large . . . five minutes before shooting time . . . never saw the animal.
—NOVEMBER 9, 2004, CAMP SHEEPSKIN REGISTER

It's grown quiet in the woods—no squirrels rustling, ravens croaking, grouse drumming, cars running, or wood being chopped. The sun has been up awhile, but a heavy mist roiling on the surface of the bog creeps up toward me. The scene becomes almost eerie, shadows become grayish, and a supernatural feeling descends over me. I think that if there is a Ghost Buck here, it will appear now.

Through the years of our hunting, the Ghost Buck continued to haunt us. It was on November 12, 1993, a wet, foggy day, that Chuck decided to explore the swamp for signs. If he found a good runway, he would carry in his portable stand and do some waiting.

He was crawling through thick firs over one of the several knolls at the end of the swamp beyond the Old Cellar when he heard a large thud beyond a dense screen of trees just ahead of him. He dropped down on one knee and looked under the trees, the only opportunity to see anything ahead. At first he didn't see anything, but then through the mist he gradually made out the dark shape of the chest of a deer and one front leg. Then the deer seemed to glide forward, like a huge shadow, revealing the shape of a massive rack. Chuck slowly raised his gun and when he looked through the scope, the deer was gone. He said later that he'd never seen such a big deer. We recorded it in the register as the monster swamp buck, but Chuck had just then become a believer in the Ghost Buck.

The next year, 1994, at the foot of Jason's Mountain, I shot the largest deer I'd ever gotten. It had nine points, an immense neck and chest, and we estimated its weight at 250 pounds. It was much larger than the big buck I had taken in Mount Vernon several years before. Cheryl was the first to arrive on the scene, and she was so overjoyed and excited that she alternated between laughing and crying. "It's the monster buck!" she exclaimed.

"Or the Ghost Buck," I said, but I wasn't convinced. I looked at the deer's hooves, and they didn't look large enough to make the tracks we'd seen in and around the swamp. I knew that this wasn't it. "More likely, it's his offspring," I said. But Cheryl still called it the monster buck, and eventually she recorded it that way in the register.

In the year 2001, we made three hunting excursions across the Old County Road below the bog, toward the Indian Pond area near where my Bennett ancestors had lived—a mountainous country with ledges, pockets for bogs, knolls of dark growth, hardwood ridges, old wood roads, and cuttings of various ages. It was here on our second day that a big (very big) doe stepped out in front of Chuck. He said she was beautiful. But what I would remember ten years later was Chuck's description of not only her size, but her color; he noted that she had a "dark gray coat."

The next hunting season, the most intriguing encounter did not involve us, but the logger who was just finishing our thinning operation. He told us excitedly that he had spotted "the biggest buck he had ever seen," while logging on the property earlier in the fall. Once again I thought of the Ghost Buck. Many years later I would wish that I'd quizzed him about the deer—how it looked, the time of day, the cover and shading where the sighting had occurred.

On November 9, 2004, Cheryl had an experience that sent a shiver through her. The report in the register referred to it as "the monster buck," but we all knew what it was about. Cheryl had just sat down in her "lucky stand" at the foot of Jason's Mountain, behind the Old Cellar, when she heard a crunch. Then, believing that the deer had caught her scent, she heard it blow. It crashed around and ran away south, around the bottom of Jason's Mountain, blowing constantly. It was five minutes before shooting hours, so she never saw the animal. "But it sounded extremely heavy and large."

At the time, I thought it was strange that she hadn't seen the deer, since it had been close enough for her to hear it blow and run. Even in the poor light that early in the day, she should have caught a glimpse of some part of a deer. I didn't voice my thoughts then, nor did I at the luncheon table that day, but once again, I was left wondering about that deer.

In 2010 I read an item in my local newspaper that gave me pause. The *Kennebec Journal* ran a story with the headline young hunter kills rare black deer. The boy was hunting with his father about forty miles northeast of Camp Sheepskin, in the town of Starks. The two were in a blind at about dusk, near the end of hunting hours, when the boy spotted a deer about 100 yards away.

What caught my attention was the next sentence: "It was a dark doe that blended in with the trees behind it. . . ." The boy shot, but it was rapidly getting dark, and they couldn't find it. "What they found the next morning, about 100 feet into the woods, shocked them, and would later surprise state biologists: a black deer." The assistant regional biologist confirmed that it was a black, or melanistic, white-tailed deer. A former deer biologist who worked for the Department of Inland Fisheries and Wildlife for twenty-seven years said that he had never heard of a black deer sighting in Maine. The department's current head deer biologist called the find "impressive [and] very rare"; he also had never heard of a black deer in his six years with the State. A black deer is much rarer than an albino or piebald deer (the latter featuring splotches of white fur).[1]

I went online to investigate melanistic deer and soon learned more. Their bodies produce too much of the dark hair and skin pigment known as melanin. White-tailed deer with this condition have black hair on the back and grayer hairs on the belly, a completely black face and ears, and a tail that is black above and white below.[2] What was particularly interesting was the color of the velvet on the racks, which tends to be

Photograph by Dean Bennett

At the edge of Sheepskin Bog—a ghost in the shadows.

brownish, but in one reported incident was gray velvet. It was also reported that not all melanistic deer are black. "Indeed, there's a wide range of shades, with some being quite black and others being more of a dirty brown or gray color."[3]

Could this be part of the mystery of the Ghost Buck? I thought back to all the signs and sightings we'd seen or heard about—the big buck in the swamp Chuck had encountered; the huge deer Cheryl had heard from her tree stand, but, despite being close, couldn't see because she thought it was in the shadows; the dark doe Chuck had seen; and other various encounters over the years. Could melanism have existed in a line of deer that had survived here, generation after generation, all these years—deer that kept to the dark swamps, receiving some camouflage protection by their coloring?

It seems very unlikely that this could be the case, considering the rarity of melanistic deer, and the fact that during so many years of hunting here, we had not had a more definitive identification of a deer with this coloring. Still, here was one confirmed in this region of western Maine, where none had ever been seen before. It's intriguing to think about, and gives us another possible explanation for the enigmatic creature that we've talked about during my lifetime, with a flicker of humor in our eyes.

Epilogue

I shift my position and turn to look again at Chuck up by the Old Cellar.

He's on his walkie-talkie, calling Cheryl. I unload my gun, hang it on the hook, unfasten my safety belt, turn around, reach up, grasp my gun, and slowly climb down from the stand. By the time I reach Chuck at the Old Cellar, Cheryl has joined him.

We start down the old road toward camp where we'll review the morning over coffee—what we've seen and heard—and then plan the rest of the day. By nightfall, we'll be dead tired and in bed early, thinking about the next day.

I know that at the end of the season, we'll leave renewed, bound a little more closely together as a family by the experiences we've shared, already anticipating the next year. That's what deer hunting has always been about for us—sharing memories of the past and making plans for the future at Camp Sheepskin.

I think my grandfather and father would agree.

Afterword

I wrote this book so that my readers would understand how hunting today has evolved from—and is a part of—the culture of many rural communities, and how it has become part of one family's traditions, helping to shape the attitudes and behavior of each successive generation.

Deer hunting, like so many other activities families can do together, is an important way my family creates and passes on from generation to generation a kind of family lore. By lore I mean the traditions, anecdotes, practical knowledge, beliefs, attitudes, values, and legends that are a part of our family's history, and help to shape our behavior. Through the years, deer hunting has brought together all of the members of my family at different times, in myriad ways, stirring our imagination, creating excitement and joy, and lifting our spirits.

For the hunters in my family, and those close to them, an approaching November hunt is a scene of increasing activity: procuring licenses and ammunition; sighting in guns and inspecting equipment; readying the camp; planning meals and buying food; assembling clothing and boots; looking for tracks and other signs of deer; poring over maps; and checking a seemingly endless number of details. During the hunting season at camp, the family becomes a team, working together, hoping at least someone will be successful in an endeavor that, despite hours of discussion, strategizing, and time in the woods, is often a matter of luck. If the hunt is successful, then group activities turn to dragging, dressing, registering, and processing. Throughout the year following the season, success leads to reliving the experience over meals of venison and desserts of mincemeat pie, showing photographs, telling stories, and planning the next season.

Through these activities, younger generations emulate role models as they experience a variety of learning situations. For example, in my hunting life, I learned that women are not excluded from hunting; gender differences don't matter. I also learned when I took my first deer what it is like to achieve a "rite of passage" in a culture that values that experience. I learned, too, that in a hunting camp, everyone shares the responsibilities inherent in close-quarters living in order for it to be smooth and efficient. Through the years, our family's hunting lore, to which I was first exposed as boy, took its place alongside other experiences and dimensions of my life.

Powerful bonds between family and friends have been forged through these shared experiences—bonds that hold us together and help direct our lives. From family hunting, we have learned standards of conduct that guide us when it comes to each other, the law, the safe handling of dangerous weapons, and the land and its wildlife. And we have learned about ourselves from others and from nature, as well as from the deer and our pursuit of them.

In my family, the bonds have held strong through my generation, my children's, and my grandchildren's. To what extent they will exist in the future, and whether they will be strong enough to ensure the survival of hunting for future generations, is a question we ask, as do many others, for we live in a world of increasingly rapid change.

We are faced with changes in lifestyle and in the economic, political, social, and natural environment in which we live. We see a rising population that is becoming more urban and mobile. Families are becoming scattered and separated by greater distances. Communications technology is occupying more of our time. Land use and land rights are being subjected to changing attitudes. People are questioning the human relationship to wild animals. There are changes in the role of government in our society as new demands are exerted. We see evidence that our economy can shift enormously with changes in outdoor recreational activities and patterns. All of these changes will have an impact on hunting, and, in turn, on the family traditions that create the family lore and bonds that will encourage future generations to hunt.

My family's experiences at Camp Sheepskin have shaped our past, our present, and our future. I hope this book may inspire your family to seek out similar adventures, and to forge strong bonds of your own.

Notes

Opening Epigraph
1. "As Time Goes By," words by Gus Kahn; words and music by Herman Hupfeld (New York: Warner Bros., Inc., 1931).

Chapter 1: The Shadagee Deer
1. Victoria Redshaw, "Taxidermy's New Role in Interiors," *The National*. See website: http://www.thenational.ae/lifestyle/house-home/taxidermys-new-role-in-interiors (accessed March 11, 2014).
2. *Report of the Commissioners of Inland Fisheries and Game for the State of Maine for the Year 1906* (Augusta: Maine State Government, 1907), 29.
3. Ibid., 23.

Chapter 2: Shadagee
1. For more information on the origin of the name *Shadagee*, see Bethel Historical Society website, Larry Glatz, "Lost in the Woods of Shadagee," *The Courier* 27, no. 1 (Spring 2003); www.bethelhistorical.org/Shadagee.html (accessed April 16, 2012).
2. Much of the history of Shadagee came from Greenwood historian, Blaine Mills, in his "History of Shadagee" (unpublished).

3. For background on Ransom Cole, see *Biographical Review: Leading Citizens of Oxford and Franklin Counties* (Boston, MA: Biological Review Publishing Co., 1897), 344–45.

4. Ernest Thompson Seton, "Whitetail Deer," reprinted from *Scribner's Magazine*, in *The Maine Sportsman* 14, no. 158 (October 1906), 53.

Chapter 3: Deer Herd

1. *Oxford Democrat*, 16 October 1906.

2. "Is the Deer Supply Decreasing?," *The Maine Sportsman* 14, no.159 (November 1906), 38.

3. Addison Emery Verrill, "Recollections of Early Settlers of Greenwood, Number Eighteen," *Oxford County Advertiser*, 18 December 1914.

4. Don C. Stanton, *A History of the White-Tailed Deer in Maine* (Augusta: Maine Department of Inland Fisheries and Game, 1963), 43–45.

5. Ibid., 37, 54.

6. Ibid., 43.

7. Gerald R. Levigne, "White-Tailed Deer Assessment Plan, 1997" (Augusta: Maine Department of Inland Fisheries and Wildlife, 1999), 52; www.maine.gov/ifw/wildlife/species/plans/mammals/white-taileddeer/speciesassessment.pdf (accessed June 22, 2012).

8. Stanton, *A History*, 42.

9. Ibid., 58.

10. Ibid., 43.

11. *Report of the Commissioners of Inland Fisheries and Game for the State of Maine for the Year 1905* (Augusta: Maine State Government, 1906).

12. Harry B. Garrison letter, *The Maine Sportsman* 14, no. 160 (December 1906).

13. Joe Wiley and Chuck Hulsey, "Living on the Edge: How Deer Survive in Winter." This article, which was published in 2010 in the newsletter of the Small Woodlot Owners Association of Maine and in *Maine Fish and Wildlife*, is available for viewing at www.mefishwildlife.com.

14. See *Guidelines for Wildlife: Managing Deer Wintering Areas in Northern, Western and Eastern Maine* (Augusta: Maine Department of Inland Fisheries and Wildlife, 2010); and Daniel Harrison and Stephen Sader, "Effectiveness of State Regulations to Protect Deer Wintering Habitats in Maine" (Orono: School of Forest Resources, Department of Wildlife Ecology, The University of Maine, 2013), PDF available at https://www.google.com/#g=effectiveness+of+state+regulations+to+protect+deer+wintering+habitats+in+maine (accessed March 12, 2014).

15. See Andrew Whitman et al., *Climate Change and Biodiversity in Maine: Vulnerability of Habitats and Priority Species*, Report SEI-2013-03 (Brunswick, ME: Manomet Center for Conservation Sciences, 2013).

Chapter 4: Predators

1. Verrill, "Recollections."

2. Mills, "History of Shadagee."

3. Ibid.

4. Ibid.

5. Ibid.

6. "USFWS Begins Review of Mountain Lion Status in East," PRNews Wire, Harrisburg, Pennsylvania, March 1, 2014; http://prnewswire.com/news-releases/

usfws-begins-review-of-mountain-lion-status-in-
east-51592522.html (accessed March 26, 2014).

7. See Francis Gould Butler, *A History of Farmington, Maine,*
1776–1885 (Farmington, ME: n.p., 1885).

8. Walter J. Jakubas, "Eastern Coyote Assessment, 1999"
(Augusta: Maine Department of Inland Fisheries and
Wildlife, 1999), 31, 56.

9. See "Chronic Wasting Disease (CWD)," from the website:
http://www.maine.gov/ifw/wildlife/disease/chronic_wast-
ing_disease.html (accessed March 26, 2014).

Chapter 5: Deer Town

1. Information on L. L. Bean in this section is from Blaine
Mills, "The Mount Abram Hotel," an essay, March 1986;
"L. L. Becomes an Orphan," article in *Oxford County Adver-*
tiser, 28 November 1884; and L. L. Bean, "L. L. Discovers
the Maine Woods," *My Story: The Autobiography of a Down*
East Merchant, 1960, *in L.L.Bean, Inc.: A Company Scrapbook*
(Freeport, ME: L.L.Bean, Inc., 2002), 2–4.

2. *Democratic News,* 25 October 1892 and 1 November 1892.

Chapter 6: The Correspondent

1. Much of the information on Lemuel Dunham is from the
website: www.megalink.net/-caronfamlmosesdunham/
ThirdGeneration.html (accessed March 29, 2012).

2. *Oxford Democrat,* 11 October 1915.

3. Ibid., 20 November 1906.

4. Greenwood, *Oxford Democrat,* 16 October 1906.

5. Ibid., 30 October 1906.

6. Ibid., 20 November 1906.

7. Ibid., 27 November 1906.

8. Ibid., 4 December 1906.

9. Ibid., 19 November 1907.

10. Ibid., 26 November 1907.

11. Ibid., 16 November 1909.

12. Ibid., 23 November 1909.

13. Ibid., 4 November 1910.

14. Ibid., 17 October 1911 and 24 October 1911.

15. Ibid., 24 October 1911.

16. Ibid., 1 November 1911, 3 December 1912, and 21 October 1913.

17. Ibid., 12 December 1911.

18. Ibid., 5 December 1911 and 10 December 1912.

19. Ibid., 9 December 1913.

20. Ibid., 10 November 1914.

21. Locke's Mills, *The Oxford Democrat*, 24 November 1914.

22. Ibid., 19 October 1915.

Chapter 7: Uncle Elmer

1. Many of the details about Elmer Kingsbury Cole were provided by Blaine Mills, researcher for the Greenwood Historical Society.

2. Greenwood, *Oxford Democrat*, 29 November 1904.

3. Ibid., 28 November 1905.

4. Lucretia Cole to Mary Cole, 26 October 1900.

5. Greenwood, *Oxford Democrat*, 9 June 1908.

6. Ibid., 17 November 1908.

7. Ibid., 2 November 1909.

8. Ibid., 1 November 1910.

9. Ibid., 5 December 1911.

10. Elmer Cole to Mary Cole Bennett, 7 November 1911.

11. Some information on Elmer Cole is from Blaine Mills and the Greenwood Historical Society, personal communication, July 2012.

Chapter 8: Into Manhood
1. For some statistics on the United States for the year 1906, see website www.csustan.edu/manage/harris/y1906.htm (accessed May 12, 2012).
2. Stanton, *A History*, 41.
3. Ibid., 53–55, 58.
4. Ibid., 36.
5. Wayne E. Reilly, "Auto Hunting Captivated Bangorians a Century Ago," *Bangor Daily News*, 11 December 2011.
6. Locke's Mills, *Oxford Democrat*, 30 November 1920.

Chapter 9: In Defense of Deer
1. *Commissioners' Report for 1906*, 27.
2. Reilly, "Auto Hunting."
3. *Report of the Commissioners of Inland Fisheries and Game for the Year 1916* (Augusta: Maine State Government, 1917).
4. Maine Department of Inland Fisheries and Wildlife History, (unpublished mimeo).
5. Stanton, *A History*, 41.
6. Ibid., 56–57.

Chapter 10: A Piece of Land
1. Locke's Mills, *Oxford Democrat*, 28 October 1923.

Chapter 11: Camp Sheepskin
1. Stanton, *A History*, 60.

Chapter 12: A Ghost in Hushed Tones

1. Stanton, *A History*, 64–66.

Chapter 16: A Hunting Pair

1. For these statistics on Maine deer hunting in 1950, see Stanton, *A History*, 63, 65, 66.

Chapter 20: Seeing Orange

1. Greenwood, *Oxford Democrat*, 29 November 1904.
2. Wayne E. Reilly, "Hunting Season Once Made the Woods a War Zone," *Bangor Daily News*, 8 November 2004.
3. "Six Killed by Hunters," *New York Times*, 31 October 1906.
4. Locke's Mills, *Oxford Democrat*, 27 October 1908.
5. Greenwood, *Oxford Democrat*, 22 December 1908.
6. Maine Department of Inland Fisheries and Wildlife History.
7. Ibid.
8. Tom Hennessey, "Only Hunters Capable of Ending Hunting Accidents," *Bangor Daily News*, 1 November 1989.
9. See a summary of Maine's test of the use of blaze orange on the number of hunting accidents in "State Reports on Tests with Fluorescent Gear," *Lewiston Evening Journal*, 21 December 1970.
10. Ibid.
11. Hennessey, "Only Hunters Capable of Ending Hunting Accidents."

Chapter 27: A Ghost in the Shadows

1. "Young Hunter Kills Rare Black Deer," *Kennebec Journal*, 9 November 2010.
2. Gino D'Angelo and John T. Baccus, "First Record of Melanistic White-Tailed Deer in Pennsylvania," *American Midland Naturalist*, 157, no. 2 (April 2007): 401.

3. Gordon Whittington, "Rarest Whitetails of All?" North American Whitetail website. www.northamericanwhitetail.com/2010/09/22/weirdwhitetails_wt_120/melanistic/ (accessed January 15, 2013).

About the Author

Dean B. Bennett at Camp Sheepskin.

D ean B. Bennett was born and raised in the town of Greenwood, Maine, in the western Maine foothills of the White Mountains. In high school he won a state contest in cabinetmaking, and after a four-year program of work and study in Portland, Maine, under the Maine Apprenticeship Program, he received his journeyman's certificate in cabinetmaking and architectural millwork. He went on receive a baccalaureate degree in industrial arts education from Gorham State Teachers College, a master's degree in science education from the University of Southern Maine, and a PhD in Resource Planning and Conservation from the University of Michigan. He taught in the Yarmouth, Maine, school system, served as the science and environmental education curriculum consultant with the

Maine Department of Education, and spent nineteen years as a professor of science education at the University of Maine at Farmington.

Much of his professional life has been devoted to teaching, and to writing and illustrating books in the fields of science and environmental education, natural history, and human relationships with nature. He received the Percival Baxter Award for Leadership in Wilderness Preservation from the Maine Chapter of the Sierra Club; the Environmental Activist Award for protection of the Allagash Wilderness Waterway from the Natural Resources Council of Maine; the Restoration Leadership Award from RESTORE: The North Woods; and the Teacher of the Year Award from Maine Audubon Society. In 2014, he and his wife, biologist Sheila K. Bennett, received the Harrison L. Richardson Environmental Leadership Award from Maine Conservation Voters.

This is his tenth book in the nature/environment field. His books include: *Maine's Natural Heritage: Rare Species and Unique Natural Features*, *Allagash: Maine's Wild and Scenic River*, *The Forgotten Nature of New England: A Search for Traces of the Original Wilderness*, *The Wilderness from Chamberlain Farm: A Story of Hope for the American Wild* for which he was awarded first place in the environment category for 2001 books by *ForeWord Magazine*, *On Wilderness: Voices from Maine* (in collaboration with Phyllis Austin and Robert Kimber), *Nature and Renewal: Wild River Valley and Beyond*, and three children's books about nature, which he also illustrated.

He enjoys playing the four-string jazz banjo, playing percussion in a steel drum band, and hiking and canoeing in the north woods of Maine with his wife.